The Ministry of All Christians

A Theology of Lay Ministry

The Ministry of All Christians

A Theology of Lay Ministry

Norman Pittenger

Morehouse-Barlow Co., Inc.
Wilton, Connecticut 06897

Morehouse-Barlow Co., Inc.
78 Danbury Road
Wilton, Connecticut 06897

ISBN 0-8192-1323-3
Library of Congress Catalog Card Number 82-62393
Printed in the United States of America

This book is dedicated
with great affection
to two dear friends,
MALCOLM and ROBERT

Preface

This book has for its subject the ministry of all Christian people. Its concern is not with the ordained ministry alone, although inevitably much will be said about that, but with the wider ministry which is a fundamental aspect in all membership in the Body of Christ which is the Church. That wider ministry, so often neglected, is now taken with utmost seriousness by Christians of every denominational background. Awareness of it and of its significance should provide the grounds for whatever may be said about those who have received ordination and hence are styled in common usage 'ministers of the Church.' My purpose is to set the work of such 'ministers' in the context of the more basic 'ministry and vocation' (to use the ancient Good Friday collect in *The Book of Common Prayer*) which is proper to 'every member of the Church.'

I believe that much of the discussion of the ordained ministry has been bedevilled by the assumption that there is a great separation between such persons and the so-called laity of the Church. But as I urge in this book, the word 'laity' means 'the people of

God'—*ho laos tou theou,* as the Greek has put it. 'The people of God' is precisely the plain New Testament way of describing *all* who are 'very members incorporate in the mystical Body of Christ.' The people of God, by virtue of their participation in the Christian community, are all of them also participant in the ministry of Christ and his priesthood. So the New Testament teaches, whether it employs the 'body' image, with St. Paul, or prefers to speak about 'the vine and its branches', as in St. John. Hence anything that is said about those who have been 'set apart', as we usually phrase it, for a specific leadership in the Church must be seen in relationship with the more general ministering function of all Christian people. When that is recognized, accepted, and implemented, many of the questions and problems commonly associated with the ordained ministry will be eased, if not entirely solved.

For our discussion this will demand that we understand that it is the people of God, members of the Body of Christ, participants in the Christian fellowship—phrase it as you will—who are the celebrants of the Church's sacraments, the proclaimers of God's Word or Self-Expression, the shepherds of Christ's flock, and above all persons who are always 'servants of the servants of God.' Inevitably in many of these areas there must be particular responsibilities and activities appropriately given to persons who are ordained for just such purposes. If this were not the case, a chaotic state of affairs would be found.

But there can never be a *separation* between the ministry belonging to all who have been baptized into Christ and that which belongs to persons who have been 'set apart' for special functions within the Church. Yet there can be a *distinction* between the two. It is strange that so many otherwise thoughtful people do not recognize the difference between 'separation' and 'distinction', although consultation of the dictionary should make that difference plain enough. To separate is to cut off or deny relationships; to distinguish is to acknowledge that in many areas this or that person may have distinctive duties and carry on a distinctive work within a larger and more inclusive whole. In New Testament language, there can be 'diversities of operation' in the Body of Christ but 'the same Spirit', as in the human body each of its members has its particular ways through which the total body is represented and its necessary functions effected.

Of course it is true that when we consider the ministry as proclamation, for example, we shall be obliged to focus attention on the work of those who have been ordained to preach, just as in discussing celebration we must speak of the leadership of such persons in the job of actual celebration. So also with respect to the pastoral or 'shepherding' aspect of ministry. But even then the point which I shall stress is that the particular duties and responsibilities of the ordained person are on behalf of, representing and functioning for, the Body as a whole. Hence I shall urge again and again that there is a profound sense in which *all* Christians do the celebrating, preaching, teaching, and shepherding, even if for orderly performance certain persons have been authorized and engraced for leadership in these ways.

It happened that during my final revision of the material contained in this book I picked up an interesting volume about Louis Evely, the famous Belgian Roman Catholic who resigned his priesthood in that communion ten or more years ago. The volume is by Neville Cryer and is entitled *Louis Evely: Once a Priest* (Mowbrays, 1980). Cryer quotes these words from Evely, written in 1971: 'Vatican II . . . began to re-orientate the Church towards its proper Christian conception by restoring to its proper place the common priesthood of all the faithful and the spiritual worship which each is called to perform in his daily life: "All their activities, prayers and apostolic engagements, their married and family life, their daily work, their spiritual, physical and leisure pursuits, if these are all lived in the Holy Spirit, become—like all the difficulties of life, provided they are borne patiently—'spiritual offerings, agreeable to God through Jesus Christ' (I Peter 2:5)"— from *Lumen Gentium,* Vatican II, section 34). Such a statement removes all division between the sacred and the profane: everything which is shot through with love is sacred.'

Evely goes on to say that the notion of the ordained minister or priest as the *sole* 'dispenser of sacred things, the mediator between the world of God and that of man, no longer has any place in the post-conciliar Church.' Rather, he says, such an ordained minister or priest is the 'enabler'—he uses here, of the ministering function of the ordained man, the French word *accoucher,* which literally (as a verb) means 'to act as a mid-wife.' Thus the ordained person is the one who, as Cryer expresses Evely's position, is 'the person who assists the rest of the People of God to become the daily priests that the Gospel expects them to be' (*op.cit.,* pp. 112f.).

All this puts simply and plainly the point which this book of mine has been written to urge and present. Furthermore, it indicates that in at least some influential Roman Catholic circles, quite as much as in Anglican, and increasingly in our own time among

Evangelical, Reformed and other so-called 'Protestant' groups, there is a remarkable movement toward what may seem a new, but is really a New Testament, conception of ministry both lay and ordained. Thus it adds weight to my own discussion, in which I portray the entire membership of the Body of Christ as engaged in celebrating, proclaiming, studying, shepherding and witnessing, in cooperation with the 'enablers' who themselves are also members of the *laos tou theou,* the 'People of God'—the 'laity' in the widest sense of that term.

In this book I shall often be found to use the words 'function' and 'functioning' in speaking of ministry. This brings us to see, as I believe, that whereas in an earlier day much talk of ministering was in static terms, or in terms of status (for the two are closely related), in our own time we think much more in terms of 'what is done'—in terms of 'function' and 'functioning.' The great philosopher Alfred North Whitehead once said that 'a thing *is* what it *does';* he rejected the idea that first we have 'something' and then, almost as an afterthought, talk of its 'doing.' As it happens, I subscribe to the wider conceptuality whose 'founding father' was Whitehead; a conceptuality which nowadays is often called 'Process Thought' with its stress on an active, energetic, dynamic, changing, societal universe. But I am sure that it is right, in any event, to interpret ministry in such terms, after 'functional' models. The New Testament does this, since its background is Jewish teaching which is essentially focussed on act and not on 'being.' What is particularly important here, to my mind, is that we can speak thus of the ministry as a 'functional' one, allowing ourselves to see that while basic functions continue down the ages, the ways in which these are performed may alter in order to meet new situations. Thus I shall urge that in ministry we have both a specific historical identity *and* changing modes for the continuation of that identity in the world.

In preparing this book I have naturally written from my own 'denominational' stance. How could I do otherwise? I happen to be an ordained priest of the Anglican Communion; I am what in the United States is called 'an Episcopalian.' Yet the material here presented has also been given, in one form or another, to conferences or assemblies of many different 'denominational' affiliations in Britain, the United States, Canada, and Australia. These have included ordained and unordained men and women belonging to the United Reformed Church in Britain; the United Methodist Church in the United States; the United Church of Christ in the

States; the 'Disciples of Christ', an American denomination; and the Roman Catholic Church both in Britain and elsewhere. It has been gratifying to find that what has been said at these several conferences or assemblies has been generously accepted and found relevant and illuminating—not least by Roman Catholics, especially if they have followed the remarkable developments in that communion since Vatican II, of which Evely's writing is representative.

If any Christians, of any communion, are helped by what is here presented to discern the way in which both ordained and unordained people are united in the basic ministry proper to Christ's Church, the time and energy spent in putting into written form what was said at the sessions I have just mentioned will be more than amply rewarded.

Norman Pittenger

King's College
Cambridge

The Church
and a Functional Ministry

In my early years as an ordained minister, I worshipped regularly in the chapel of the theological school where I taught. This was the General Theological Seminary of the Episcopal Church in the United States; its chapel was known as 'the Chapel of the Good Shepherd.' Slightly above and behind the altar or communion table in that chapel was a statue representing Jesus as the Good Shepherd, the name by which (according to St. John's Gospel) he called himself when he wished to indicate his concern and his care for the men and women and children to whom he had been sent by God his heavenly Father, among whom he lived and worked, taught and acted, and for whom he was prepared to die a cruel death so that they 'might have life and have it more abundantly.'

I suppose that this explains why I have always thought of my own ordained ministry, and in consequence of all ministering work in the Christian Church, as a sharing in that care and concern. The continual placarding before my eyes of the Good Shepherd made me feel that the function of Christian ministering is nothing other and nothing less than a readiness to be open to, and readiness to be used by, the One who *is* the Good Shepherd.

As I shall urge in this book, I believe that the whole Church is a ministering representative of Jesus Christ. Furthermore, I am convinced (and this also I shall be urging) that while there is a distinction between ordained ministry and that which is proper to those who are unordained, there is no separation between them. Hence *all* share in ministry; and they share this as representing and acting for the Good Shepherd in *his* ministry. In the recently released American Prayer Book—'the new book', as it is often called—I have found a splendid statement which is relevant here. There is a 'new Catechism' in that book; and in this catechism the following questions and answers appear:

'Question: Who are the ministers of Christ?

'Answer: The ministers of Christ are lay-persons, bishops, priests, and deacons.

'Question: What is the ministry of the laity?

'Answer: The ministry of lay-persons is to represent Christ and his Church; to bear witness to him wherever they may be; and, according to the gifts given them, to carry on Christ's work of reconciliation in the world; and to take their place in the life, worship, and governance of the Church.'

The catechism goes on to speak also of the duties of bishops, priests and deacons, saying that each of these is also 'to represent Christ and his Church' in appropriate and designated fashion.

The motif of 'Good Shepherd' may be difficult for many today in our highly technological and urban society; yet this term has both biblical precedent and deep meaning. Certainly it is easy to see how silly was the suggestion made some years ago that for 'pastoral' we should substitute 'technological'; and that one whose job is to teach 'pastoral theology' should occupy instead a chair of 'technological theology'!

There is another difficulty in the use of the words 'pastor' or 'shepherd' and in the use of the idea of 'shepherding' as characteristic of ministering in the Christian Church, whether it be ordained or unordained. After all, it may be said, such language and such an idea suggest that those whom one serves, God's human children, are like 'silly sheep.' For many of our contemporaries, the notion that other people are 'sheep' and need 'shepherding' carries with it the implication that they are not only 'silly' but also irresponsible and lacking genuine understanding of themselves. Doubtless there are some clergymen and laypeople who have this mistaken view. And doubtless there are men and women who like 'to be told', so that they are not burdened with responsibility and need not bother to understand their own status as children of God who should not be treated like immature infants. But granted the existence of such persons, surely the duty of Christian men and women is to help them to grow to mature responsibility. Each of us, whether ordained or unordained, should do all in our power to further such growth in Christ, to the end that our sisters and brothers may come to full maturity.

For myself, the picture of the Lord we worship as the 'Good Shepherd' carries with it both the authority of the Christian tradition and the validation of the New Testament witness. It suggests the loving concern for others which is at the heart of Christian faith in God as God is disclosed 'for us men and for our salvation' in the manhood of Jesus Christ. And when these ideas are applied to the Church's ministering work, they have (for me, anyway) an evocative power even today. In any event, in this book I intend to use that image again and again as I try to discuss the various aspects of the common Christian priesthood in Christ. And insofar as we turn, from time to time, to the *ordained* minister, call him what we wish—priest, pastor, rector, vicar, curate, or anything else—we shall find that the image of shepherd will provide food for thought and inspiration for action. In the total life of the Church of Christ, their function is especially to seek to bring the nonordained to that full maturity of which I have just spoken. Thus all of us will come to be men and women who through our membership in Christ's Body the Church are empowered and strengthened in our vocation.

In respect to those ordained persons, I find it helpful to recall something said by a holy and humble clergyman of my acquaintance. He was preaching to a large group of young men who were in a theological college training for the ordained ministry. He pointed out that just as Christ himself was 'a priest after the order of Melchisedec' (the passage from Hebrews was his text for his sermon), so also Christ was the Shepherd of God's children and was thus 'a servant after the order of the Good Shepherd.' The Good Shepherd 'gave his life for the sheep'; he was most certainly willing to be called their 'servant' and to minister to them in that humbling capacity. We may recall that in the old Ordinal in *The Book of Common Prayer,* there are fine words in which the ordinand is told that those who receive holy orders are to be, not only 'messengers, watchmen, and stewards of the Lord', not only 'to teach and to premonish, to feed and provide for, the Lord's family', but also 'to seek for Christ's sheep that are dispersed abroad, and for his children who are in the midst of this naughty world, that they may be saved through Christ for ever.' The words may be antiquated; they may sound quaint to our modern ears. Yet they say something very important about the nature and work of *all* ministry in Christ's Church, not least in the unashamed use of the phrase 'Christ's sheep.'

In still other ancient words, the ordained minister is said to be concerned 'to minister the doctrine and sacraments, and the discipline of Christ, as the Lord hath commanded.' The way in which that minister will perform the task will naturally be in accordance with the particular understanding which is found in the 'denomination' or Christian group to which the ordained person belongs. It will also be carried out today in a fashion different in many ways from that which was appropriate in an earlier age—'new occasions teach new duties', the poet has written. But one constant factor in ministry is the caring or concern for others which is required in any and every age; and about various aspects of that caring or concern we shall be speaking in this book. Anybody who has eyes open, ears attentive, and the wit to comprehend will see readily that this constant factor, in its varying expressions, must be adapted to the changing circumstances and situations in which men and women find themselves. Yet at the same time the care and concern will always be through proclamation of the gospel of Christ, the administration of or sharing in the sacramental rites of the Church, the guidance provided for Christian living, as well as the help given to people in their moments of anguish. These can never change. And it is to these that the Christian, whether ordained or unordained, is called, although obviously the way in which the ordained person functions will be in many ways distinct from, yet never separated from, the way in which the unordained or lay person must act.

I cannot emphasize too strongly the point just made: that there are indeed distinctions but no separation as between ordained and lay ministry. About this I shall speak in the remainder of the present opening chapter. In later chapters I shall turn to the meaning of the faith which all Christian people profess and to which they are called to witness publicly; the work of the minister, ordained by the Church, to celebrate the sacraments, yet without for a moment forgetting that the nonordained also have their part and place in that celebration; the teaching of Christian belief and the Christian moral stance, in which all Christ's people must have a share; the necessity for learning, through a scholarly approach, again by all

Christians, to the Christian tradition into which we are baptized and in which we stand—although only a few will be called to a specifically 'academic' kind of scholarship; the pastoral care of others, in their joys and in their sorrows; and finally, with an apology for a word whose use is often attached solely to ordained persons, the way in which 'every member of Christ, in his [or her] vocation and ministry', must be 'a man' or 'a woman' who is truly 'of God.'

Before we turn to the consideration of the nature of ministry, however, I feel it incumbent upon me to speak somewhat personally. As one whose entire adult life has been spent in teaching in theological schools or colleges or (more recently) in the supervision of those engaged in theological research in a university, I may be regarded as incompetent to discuss the very practical ministering which is the given task of the nonacademic Christian. Is it not improper for a person like me to attempt this task? I hope not; and this hope is strengthened by two considerations. First, like every one who has been baptized into membership in the community of Christian faith, worship and life, I have known—although often I have seriously failed in—the responsibility to care for others, within and without the institutional Church. Thus I have some awareness of the wider ministry which appertains to all Christian people through their belonging to the Body of Christ. Secondly, a person who like me has exercised his ordained ministry almost entirely in guiding those who are themselves to be ordained, or are already ordained, is not quite so aloof from concrete pastoral concerns as sometimes is assumed. After all, a teacher does have, or ought to have, what used to be called 'the care of souls.' Obviously some who teach are so narrowly concerned with academic matters that they forget or neglect this. But it remains the fact that people like myself are usually interested in their students. We too have been 'called, tried, examined, and known to have such qualities as are requisite for so weighty a work' as ministering, to use once more the splendid language of the Prayer Book Ordinal. Doubtless we fail, again and again, to implement in practice what we have been ordained to be and to do. None the less, nobody who is thus devoted to teaching theological students can fail to remind himself of his responsibility; nobody in this work of teaching need regard himself as very different from others whose labors are in more immediately practical activity in the life of the Christian community.

This, then, is why I venture to write this book—not for fellow-academics but for the generality of Christian people, ordained and unordained. I write it in the conviction that we all of us need to meditate often and to consider deeply what are the several areas of Christian concern. And perhaps an approach to such matters from one who by specific vocation has a theological interest in ministering may not be lacking in value. Is it not sometimes true that discussion of these questions can be altogether *too* practical? That is to say, it can be (in one sense, anyway) somewhat *unprincipled*, precisely because it fails continually to return to 'first principles', to the basic affirmations and convictions which are distinctively and specifically Christian.

We now turn to consider the nature of ministry. Logically, we should begin by an investigation of the history of that central aspect of Christ's Church, with attention to its New Testament origins, its development from primitive times to the emergence of fairly well-defined 'orders' within the wider ministerial reality of the community, and the ways in which, later on, distinctions were made as to the responsibilities or duties of those who had been admitted into the ordained ministry. But this is not the place for such an investigation. I shall confine myself to ministry today, recognizing of course that 'holy orders' (as many Christian communions would define the ordained ministry) have a long and complicated history.

But first of all, such 'holy orders' have significance only in the context of 'holy order'—that is to say, in the broader ordering of the life of the Christian Church as a whole, in which each and every member has a share and through which each and every member is called to a ministering function. As I said above, the Church is the 'People of God', *ho laos tou theou*, as the Greek puts it. Thus all of us belong to the 'laity'. The distinction between those who are and those who are not ordained must not be taken to imply that the unordained are denied a responsible participation in the general ministering activity of the community. From the New Testament portrayal of the Christian fellowship, 'fellowship in the Holy Spirit', we can readily see that sense can be made of the 'office and work' of ordained persons only when and as they are set in the wider context, where every Christian is both 'under orders' and also himself or herself 'ordered' toward the service of those who are God's children. Each of us is a 'servant of the servants of God', the fine title which has been given to the Bishop of Rome. Not only are ordained persons such servants; all of us are servants both of each other and of the vast number of men and women who are not enrolled members of the Church and hence may not be in any obvious sense 'Christians.'

Some Christian communions have tended, as a matter of historical development, to separate the ordained from the unordained; and to do this by a very great gulf. They have often been prepared to speak of the 'teaching Church', by which they mean the ordained ministry in its hierarchical arrangement, and of the 'learning Church', by which they mean the great mass of unordained Christian believers. Other Christian communions have tended, in their historical development, to make no genuine distinction between unordained and ordained persons. For these communions, the latter are called to serve as leaders of the former, chosen by the general body of believers to act for them but with no special functions which, in the ordering of the Church's existence, are given them by God in Christ through the Body of Christ.

But one of the remarkable phenomena of our time has been a new slant on the ministry which more closely resembles the New Testament picture. Thanks to this, the former tendency, to separate ordained and unordained, has been modified enormously by the keen recognition of 'the priesthood of the laity', the whole people of God; while the latter tendency, refusing any genuine distinctions of function between ordained and unordained, has also been modified by the recognition that there are particular responsibilities which the ordained are to assume precisely because they are representative of, function for, and carry on certain essential duties which, in the last resort, appertain to the whole people of God in its ministering work. The former position has been associated hitherto with the so-called 'Catholic communions'; the latter with the so-called 'Reformed communions', and especially with a congregational or 'independent' church polity. Perhaps the Holy Spirit has been at work in both, in these latter days, to bring them closer together, to value the emphasis which each of them has made during its history, and to prepare us all for a deeper and surely a more basically Christian understanding of all ministering in the Church.

I believe that a properly scriptural view of the meaning of Christian ministry requires that we begin our discussion by seeing that *all* priesthood—and all ministry in every aspect—is derivative from the one essential priesthood which is that of Jesus Christ himself. *He* is the one true Priest, which is to say that in Christian faith it is he who stands from God to humankind and from humankind to God. He is the mediator, not as if he were some *tertium quid* between God and human existence but because precisely in him our faith sees One who is both the *organon* or instrumental agent for God's coming to us in a definitive and decisive fashion and also the instance in human existence in which adequate and proper response is made, from the human side, to that divine prevenience or priority. God to mankind; mankind to God: in the event we indicate when we say 'Jesus Christ' Christian faith sees the classical instance, the specific case, where this two-way movement is (so to say) 'clinched' and focussed.

But the Christian Church has understood itself, from St. Paul's day onward, to be the Body of Christ. It is his agent in the world, concerned to do his work and to manifest his activity (and hence his real presence) to the human race. The Church is portrayed in the New Testament as like a physical body or like a vine with its branches; it is not talked about as if it were merely an organization like some society or club or group. Of course it is organized; any agency in the world must of necessity have such a social pattern if it is to continue in doing its job. But at its heart it is organically one with its Lord; and its ministering is his gift, to be received and implemented. Thus, if Christ is the one true Priest, the Church has its priesthood, too. We may say, we ought to say, that its existence is to act for and represent the Lord's priestly work. Hence it has both a real *and* a derived priesthood, originatively and essentially Christ's own priesthood delegated to the Body which is his Church.

The priesthood of the Church consists in its self-identification with the abiding reality of Christ's own sacrificial action in the world. This the Church proclaims; with this the Church, in its inner existence, seeks to be one. This expresses itself towards God in self-offering and toward God's children in devoted service. As an Anglican divine wrote, at the turn of the century, 'the powers, the privileges, the capacities,' of those who are ordained are precisely and exactly 'the powers, the privileges, the capacities of the Body as a whole'—and these are from Christ, of Christ, and for Christ. Thus the character and responsibility which may be attributed to ordained persons in the Church cannot be 'antithetical or inconsistent' with the total ministerial reality of the Body of Christ; rather, they are 'correlative and complementary' and the two together (ordained and unordained) must be understood as 'mutually indispensable ideas.' The writer whom I have been quoting was R. C. Moberly and his whole discussion in the book *Ministerial Priesthood* is notable for its clarity and discernment.

There is indeed a distinctive functioning proper to those who are ordained; but that is not something separate from or utterly in contrast to what is true of the laity *in toto;* above all, it is not a negation of, but a particular action for, the priesthood which belongs to those who have not been ordained yet by virtue of their membership in the Body of Christ share in the Church's priestly nature. Somebody who has been ordained has the privilege of representing, in an 'enabling' capacity, the ministering priesthood of the Church; such a person functions for the Church, so that what is done in the community may be done 'decently and in order', as St. Paul put it. The ordained person represents the priestly Church and in so doing represents Christ *in* his Church.

Thus all ministry is ultimately Christ's ministry, carried on in and by his Body the Church and directed, like his own historical ministry, toward God and toward the world. Nobody who has been ordained stands alone or acts alone, as if his ministry was of and for and by himself. The ordained person stands for, and acts on behalf of, the whole Body of Christ, through which Body the Lord has chosen to carry on his work in the world. This is the deeply scriptural, historically catholic, and genuinely 'reformed' way of thinking about ministry; and it rests back upon the convictions to which in the last few paragraphs we have given attention. And let us notice here that to speak about 'the priesthood of the laity' is not to speak in individualistic terms. As the New Testament makes clear, this priesthood (even when it is presented as 'the priesthood of believers') is a social affair. It has to do with the social reality which is the Church's essential nature.

Hence an ordained minister is a representative under-shepherd for the Good Shepherd. Such is one who does not and cannot act of by, or for self. All is of God in Christ, by God in Christ, and for God in Christ; and because the Christian community is indeed Christ's Body, his family, his flock, all is of, by, and for the Church. It is scandalous for anyone to speak of 'his' ministry; it is always, for the ordained as well as for those who are unordained yet sharers in the Church's priesthood, *Christ's* ministry and hence the *Church's* ministry, concerned to bring Christ to the world and the world to Christ, in sacrifice and service.

In what has gone before in this discussion, I have sought to undercut the conventional Protestant-Catholic division by taking as a starting-point the general picture which the New Testament gives us and which in the earliest days of the Church's history was continued. Such a conception of ministry is *functional.* Ministry is understood and exercised in terms of what it is here *to do* rather than in terms of a supposed status which attaches to it as such. That is exactly what we should expect, if we have regard for the way in which the Bible speaks of God, of God's activity in the world, and of the human response to that activity. Interestingly enough, in our own day precisely such emphasis on functioning, in every area of human life, is to be found. Nowadays people think in terms of what is to be done, by whom, and how, rather than in terms of position or rank alone. This change has come about because the world is seen as being dynamic, processive, and societal. This is why contemporary theology increasingly talks about divine activity and movement in relationship and love, much more than did our ancestors who were the 'victims' (if I may put it so) of a 'substantial' view of things.

But then what *is* this function of ministry? In St. Paul's words in II Corinthians, it is to be 'the helper of our joy', our joy in Christ and in our life in God through him. There are various channels through which that help is given, to the end that those who belong to the Christian community may be established in the faith in which by baptism they have come to stand, may grow daily in God's grace, and may witness to the world that he is indeed 'mighty to save.' Thus a minister of the Church, whether ordained to serve as a specific representative agent for the Church's wider priesthood, or unordained but still participant in that priesthood and hence herself or himself genuinely a minister, is to be a personalized agent for the bringing to God's children of new life in Christ, which is life in Love (notice that the noun here is capitalized, to indicate that I am speaking of *God*) and hence is also life in love (lower-case 'l', to indicate that I am now speaking of human relationships). This ministry is to every man and woman and child, in every place and situation and circumstance.

If what has been said so far is true, then we shall do well to meditate often on the humility which must mark the life and attitude of both the ordained and the unordained. For if one is indeed to function as a representative of the living Christ, he or she is acting on behalf of that Lord in his living Body; hence he or she must be humble in the presence of so great a responsibility. We can make no claim for ourselves. We can only be grateful that we have been given the privilege of service in this capacity. Furthermore, we shall do well to consider the responsibility which this entails. 'Responsibility' can mean two things, both of them important, both of them relevant at this point. First of all, the word can mean that a *response* is made to the specific vocation which is proper to each of us; and second, such response demands *accountability*, so that the vocation is exercised in the right fashion. The lay minister, the unordained man or woman, *and* the ordained person as well, is always to act, to live, to speak, so far as in her or him lies, so that the Good Shepherd's own caring ministry may be reflected and represented. Our Lord came 'to seek and to save those who were lost'—the bewildered, lonely, unloved, loveless, maltreated, neglected, forgotten sons and daughters of men. He thought not of his own glory but of the good of those whom he came to serve. He gave his life for them, even unto the death of the Cross, so that they might 'live through him.' This also is to be true of those who minister, in whatever capacity; they are to seek to function, however imperfectly, inadequately, and defectively that may be done, for God in Christ.

Unless this quality of true representation comes clear through the lives of those who are thus 'of Christ' they will be unprofitable servants. The ordained person has a particularly difficult role here, for others tend to look to those who have been given a specific function on behalf of the whole Body. Each must seek to measure himself by that call; each is unworthy both of the call which has been accepted and in the exercise of that specific ministry. The chief concern, therefore, for both ordained and unordained, is that one's heart be pure—and this means, as the great Danish thinker Kierkegaard so vividly put it, that one 'wills one thing.' That 'one thing' is sacrifice and service. Here again the pattern of the Good Shepherd is entirely plain.

I have not hesitated to use the 'Shepherd' image, despite the misunderstandings which for some may be attached to it. False notions must be carefully avoided; yet we can profit greatly by seeing how Jesus spoke of the work of shepherding without the slightest trace of condescension or contempt for those whom he called his 'sheep.' What is more, he was willing to 'lay down his life for the sheep.' And as St. Bernard wrote in the Middle Ages, what matters most is 'not so much the death as the willingness of him who died.' By this willing, our Lord has brought to humankind the possibility, indeed the very actuality, of newness of life in faith and hope and love. Every man and woman and child is intended by God to share in that newness. To have some part in the ministering task of making such 'newness of life' available to others is a privilege beyond measure, yet it is a privilege granted to all members of the Christian community or fellowship. Nobody can contemplate such a privilege without a shattering of our all-too-human pride.

Christian Faith and Human Life

Each Christian is a minister of Christ in the world; each is a servant of Christ's servants; each shares in the priesthood which is proper to the Church as the Body of Christ. *Some* have been ordained to a specific function in that Church, to stand for, to represent, and to act as the Church's designated agent in the performance of those duties which require an appointed person for doing them. *All* are under-shepherds of the Good Shepherd; *some* have been ordained to fulfill particular and important responsibilities on behalf of, but not in contradiction to, the rest of the Church's membership.

This was the view which we expounded in the last chapter. Now we must turn to the question: what is the *raison-d'être*, the meaning and significance, of the Church itself? What is the purpose of the Church, to the doing of which it is dedicated and for the reality of which it is here in the world?

First of all, then, the Church is in the world *to do something*. It has its functional character, like everything else in a dynamic, processive, societal creation—in a world which is being created, for that word 'creation' should not be used only in the past tense, as if it had been done ages ago. The world is being created, in a continuous process, by a living God who intimately and unfailingly relates himself to a world which he loves and for which he has a purpose. Thus the Church *is* 'mission', as so often we have heard in recent years. It does not merely 'have a mission'; it *is* 'mission', here in the world to do something which is of enormous importance. Awareness of this helps us to grasp the truth that the Church cannot be defined or described in static and 'fixed' terms. The Church, as 'mission', is itself a social process in a world which is also a social process. But in that world the Church's function is specific to itself; it will not do to look at it as if it were just another one of the many groupings, organizations, or associations which exist for carrying on the ordinary activities proper to human existence. As I urged in the last chapter, the Church of course is a social phenomenon; but in its own self-understanding, in its inner existence, it is much more than that.

So it is that we must say, in the second place, that the Church exists *for the gospel of Jesus Christ;* indeed, for the gospel which *is* Jesus Christ. This is the basic *raison-d'être* of the Church, although its work in the world is effected through various activities: celebrating, proclaiming, and witnessing to what in Christ God has 'determined, dared, and done' (in Christopher Smart's splendid words). That is why we must now ask: what *is* that gospel?

Briefly, the gospel is the good news that Jesus Christ has come and lived and taught and acted and suffered and died and has been 'raised from the dead'; that he is now a continuing power and presence in the world and that because of him two things have happened. First, a disclosure has been made, in concrete historical fact, of God's nature and his way of acting in the creation. And secondly, through this event men and women, who respond to it in faith, are caught up into a new life. The disclosure reveals that God is nothing other than sheer love; the result, for those who respond, is the possibility of life 'in love'—and this means not only loving relationships with one another but a sharing in the very life of the God who *is* Love. Such a new life is called 'life in Christ', in the phrase which St. Paul uses over and over again. But 'life in Christ' is nothing other than life in the God who is active in Christ; hence it is 'life in Love'—with an upper-case 'L' since we are talking about God with us and in us, through the reality of the divine activity in Jesus Christ. The result of the event of

Christ, in all its fulness, is a new community of love and in love; and that community is the Church as Christ's Body in the world.

So much is, or ought to be, plain enough to every Christian. This gospel explains the existence of the Church, even as it is the Church which both witnesses for and serves as instrument of that gospel. If we are to understand ministry aright, we must begin with the gospel and its implications. To say that, however, is to point to theological matters. The gospel itself is not a theological proposition, of course; none the less, the gospel entails theological affirmations or it lacks firm foundations. Men and women are more or less rational creatures, who have a capacity to understand and relate their experience to wider concerns; and hence they must think about what has happened to them in their response to the event of Jesus Christ. If the gospel, responded to by God's children, had no such basically theological implications, it would be mere words about human experience or mere reference to supposed historical occurrences; it would lack a 'world view' which is grounded in the gospel's reality and hence is specifically and definitively Christian. For Christianity is no mere speculation, nor is it just an interesting and inspiring theory; it is firmly based in historical fact as that fact is known by men and women who have said their dedicated 'yes' to its impact upon them.

To many people the notion of a 'simple gospel' makes an appeal; they feel that talk about theology, or the rational ordering in a coherent and consistent pattern of that which constitutes the Christian message, is an unnecessary complication. But thoughtful people should recognize that to talk in that fashion is to play straight into the hands of obscurantism and superstition. If the gospel of Christ is to commend itself, as surely it must, to the minds of men and women, as well as to their will and emotions, it requires a theological understanding of its implications. Therefore we must now consider the theology which is implicit in the gospel proclamation and the response made to it through the centuries by people who have found it to be 'the truth of God unto salvation.' And I begin by saying that Christianity is 'all one thing' and not a collection of diverse beliefs and ideas.

To put it very briefly, the *one thing* is the new life in Christ which is given to us as we respond in faith to the good news of God's action towards humankind in Jesus Christ—and, when we have thus responded, proceed to live in the confidence which it brings to us. Everything that is essential or important in the total

Christian enterprise plays into that new life or flows from it. Anything that does not play into it or flow from it is either unnecessary or unimportant. The distinguished German-American theologian Paul Tillich used to contend that what he styled 'the new being in Christ' was the ultimate criterion for Christian life, worship, and thought. I believe that he was getting at the truth; but I think that his point would be better phrased if we spoke, as I have just done, of 'life in Christ', which is nothing other than 'life in Love (and note again the capital 'L', since I am here referring to God, known in the event of and response to Jesus Christ, as the cosmic Lover whose scope is always universal and the application of that scope is always particular). But to say 'life in Love', in terms of the event of Jesus Christ, is at the same time to recognize that the quality of that 'Love' is given in terms of Jesus Christ and his impact upon humankind.

Having said all this, we must now proceed to consider *the faith* which comes into existence through the reality of our response *in faith*. By my play on words here, I am trying to indicate that there is indeed something which may properly be called 'the Christian faith'; I am also implying that this faith gives us a 'world view' and that it has its significance in that it is the natural, we might even say inevitable, result of the stance of faith—that is, of the trust or commitment or (as the Latin has it) *fiducia* in God known through Christ. It is that stance, the faith or commitment of the genuinely believing man or woman, which 'justifies' us. It does this through assuring us, and doing this more than merely verbally or intellectually, that we are accepted by God and hence are able to accept ourselves and to accept others. Through this faith, in the profound sense just given it, we are enabled to come to *the faith,* which is the Church's faith and is also to be our own. That Christian faith is set forth in the convictions or affirmations which are at the heart of the ongoing Christian tradition, which animate the Christian community, and which thoughtful Christian people attempt to state, however inadequately this may be, in a theology or organic pattern of truth.

I myself should wish to state this central faith in the following fashion: God, who is the center of it all, is living, dynamic, active, and related to the world. God is supremely worshipful because perfect in love and wisdom, utterly unsurpassable by anything other than the divine reality itself. God is the final dependability; God is the chief explanatory principle, although not the only one, nor the only 'cause' in the world since. There is a relative creaturely freedom and creaturely causation throughout all that which is not God. This must be acknowledged if creaturely existence, human or natural, has any meaning. But God is not only the chief explanatory principle; God is also what I may call the chief 'affective principle.' By this I mean that God is not remote and unconcerned nor is God so much self-existent that other realities make no difference to the divine reality. On the contrary, we ought to insist upon God's being affected or influenced by what goes on in the world. God is 'the fellow-sufferer who understands', in Whitehead's great phrase. God receives, accepts, and takes into his own life, and God also employs for his master-purpose of love, what is done by the 'creatures'—by men and women, to be sure, but also by everything else as well.

To say that God creates—and that verb should be used (as I urged earlier) in the present tense, not in the past alone, since God is *always* creatively active—is to say that God manifests and expresses the divine nature in act; he is *self-expressed,* and he is *self-expressive.* It is God's very self which acts, not some secondhand agency or instrument.

Now when we say 'self-expression' we are pointing to the mystery of God's boundless self-giving. So great and inexhaustible in this self-giving, which is nothing other than Love-at-work, that we dare to assert (if we are Christians) that such self-giving or self-expression is itself the reality of God; it *is* God vis-à-vis the created world. This is why in Christian thought there has been much talk about the Eternal Word, the *Logos* as the Greek New Testament has it, as being integral to the divine life. St. John's Gospel speaks of this: 'In the beginning was the Word, and the Word was with God, and the Word was truly divine [God].' 'All things were made by [or through] that Word', John goes on to tell us; God creates and reveals and redeems through his Word or Self-Expression. Which is to say, God is the active and acting Lover who always and faithfully moves out of himself to establish love in the creation and to win love from men and women who are being made for exactly that purpose.

You and I are God's children. Our creaturely potentiality is to become responding personalized agents for the divine Love. But only when that potentiality is quickened and brought to genuine actualization do we become truly and fully human. The basic trouble with us is that we are not only feeble and fallible but also wilful and wrongly-centered in our own will and way. This is our human condition; and whatever we do or say or think which follows from this 'wrongness' is sin. To this we shall return. For the moment let me emphasize that in Jesus Christ, where God's Word or Self-Expression was given definitive human enactment, we have been granted a vision of God's *express* Image. Thus, as Martin Luther used to put it, Jesus Christ is 'the Proper Man'—human existence in him is human existence as it is intended by God to be. And this is so, because in and through him God is signally active and hence signally present, in a decisive and focal manner. He is *the* Son of God. This is the indemonstrable but unavoidable testimony of Christian faith, the affirmation which makes men and women specifically Christian people.

Yet, whatever some misguided people may have thought, Jesus Christ is not the *only* place of God's activity. He does not confine the working of the Word in the world; rather, he defines it. He is not the supreme anomaly; he is the classical instance. To put it in this way is not for a moment to reduce him to the level of 'mere humanity'; for there is no such thing. Each one of us has his or her own speciality; each has his or her 'importance.' Nor does speaking of Jesus as 'classical instance' make him only a very splendid example of God's general immanence in the world. On the contrary, it raises the potentiality in each and every man and woman and relates this to what God has 'determined, dared, and done' (as we saw that 'Mad Kit Smart' once said) in *this* place, through *this* Man, and once and for all. *Once,* because it took place, with the speciality which attaches to every historical occurrence, in an historical personality which like all historical personalities has its 'uniqueness'; *for all,* because its purpose is to provide the 'new and living way' into fellowship with the divine Father of us all, for everyone of God's children. Thus in Christ that which is potential in all men and women by virtue of the fact of their creation is made actual in concrete human life by virtue of the *new* creation in Christ. *In* him we see the express Image of God; *by* him, we are empowered or enabled to be conformed to that Image. The ancient Fathers of the Church put this in a splendid phrase: *filii in Filio,* 'we become sons in the Son.' In unprecedented measure and with ever-renewing energy, the deep of God which was at work in him calls forth the response from the deep in us; and it does this so profoundly and so personally that the response is not simply our own human striving (although it *is* that), but is also such striving now made possible and fruitful by 'the operation of the Holy Spirit', God's own working in us. So the

Holy Spirit may rightly be called *God's Self-Response,* just as the Word is God's Self-Expression.

The reader of these paragraphs may say that this is theology; it is, indeed. But it is also vital religion. We are talking of the full-orbed triunitarian picture of God, known and adored as the Father who is sheer Love; as the Word (or the Son) who is that Love Self-Expressed; and as the Spirit who is that Love Self-Responsive. And we may even dare to say that genuine Christian life is nothing less than our being caught up into this triune life of God himself; and, being thus caught up, being securely established forever in that life.

Let us be clear that the Christian centuries have not turned a good man, Jesus, into the 'God-Man', as used to be said by some critics. What they *have* done is discover in and through the full and complete (hence timed and spaced) humanity of Jesus the very activity (and hence the very presentness) of God—the presence *because* of the activity, as I should wish to phrase it. We may not (and I do not) much like the word 'God-Man'; but we must acknowledge that it was, for the ancient theologians of the Church, the way of saying what I have just been urging about the significance of Jesus Christ for those who are of *the* faith because they have had their own faith (commitment and trust) in Jesus Christ validated in the experience of newness of life and 'joy and peace in believing.'

In making this affirmation of faith, which is in no sense a denial of the wider operation of God's action in the world, the ancient theologians believed that they had stated the clue to *what everything is about.* Here was the now-revealed secret of existence divine and human, disclosed to *some* for the benefit of *all.* And that clue is simply love, as I have continually emphasized. It is Love divine; as Dante wrote in the conclusion of The Divine Comedy, 'the Love that moves the sun and the other stars'; it is this same Love that moves the hearts of men and women and that matters most to all of us. This is why the English recusant poet Robert Southwell could pen those marvellous words: 'Not where I breathe, but where I love, I live.' Equally right, and speaking from the heart of ordinary men and women, is the saying (at which cynics are likely to sneer, alas!), 'This love is greater than either of us or both of us together.' Here ordinary human loving is taken as a clue to divine Love. Many theologians have thought any such analogy blasphemous, but the gospel narratives portray Jesus himself as using it; and the hearts of men and women, without sophistication as they usually are, declare it to be true. Likewise true are the words of a popular song of a few years ago, 'You're nobody till somebody loves you.' All this common feeling, as well as the religious affirmation about which we are speaking, receives validation, vindication, and vividness in Jesus Christ, where 'Somebody'—namely God himself—is shown to have loved us poor children of his. And our response in faith, which is commitment and trust, is to *that* Love, greater indeed than anything human, which completes and corrects our feeble and defective human loving, which clarifies the past, illuminates the present, and opens up new and astounding possibilities for the future.

So far as we humans are concerned, this divine Love both ennobles us and shames us. We are being created, day by day and year by year, to become created, finite, mortal, and certainly limited lovers. Yet as an experienced fact, our defection is what most strikes us when we happen to be honest about ourselves. Not only are we frustrated in our loving; we are also distorted and twisted in it. We love the wrong things or we love the right things in the wrong way. But we could not live at all wthout love. So St. Augustine prays to God that he will 'order [our] loving'—our human loving is distorted and it needs to be set right or properly 'ordered.' The disordering or distortion is our sin; the right ordering is our salvation, which only God can provide.

Because of this disordering, we are estranged and alienated from God who *is* Love; we are also alienated and estranged from our fellows and from our own true and divinely-intended personhood. We are in a situation which is 'all messed up', as someone has phrased it. The cause of that appalling fact, which we cannot alter by our own efforts, is in the way in which we are all of us caught in the total human situation, through millenia of wrong-choosing with its consequences. But the gospel is the proclamation that for us men and women, where we are and as we are, the manifestation of the express Image of God in Jesus Christ carries with it the 'translation' of sinful people into 'the kingdom of his dear Son, in whom we have redemption, even the forgiveness of our sins.' We are thereby made to be what God always has meant us to be, by God's creative act in the first instance and now by his redeeming love in the concrete event of Jesus Christ in the second instance. We can be knit together in a redeemed community, planted in the life of God in Christ, nourished and strengthened through his grace, and become in fact what in principle we have always been: the sons and daughters of God, after the pattern and in the power of him who is 'First-born Son.' We are made *free*.

Something like this, to which I have given several pages, is a theological way of stating *the* faith which is the response *in* faith that the proclamation of the gospel is intended to evoke. Notice that it is a triunitarian faith, as I have urged; notice too that it is concerned with God as not only creating us, as not only redeeming us, but as also crowning in us his purpose which was 'from the beginning', before ever we humans sinned. His abiding intention is to bring his children into the closest conceivable union with himself. True God acted in, hence was present through, a True Man, to bring us to himself and to make us fully human and therefore free people. And God was *in us* too, working by the Holy Spirit to enable our response in faith, to give us hope, and to fill us with his own faithful and unfailing love.

But it may be asked, What has all this theology to do with the lives of ordinary men and women? What does it do to and for those lives? We have already seen something of the answer to these questions. It is the Church's responsibility, as it is the privilege of Christian people, to labour under God, to the end that just such ordinary men and women, who do the work of the world, can find meaning in their daily duties and become what I have earlier called 'personalized instruments' for God the great 'Lover of souls.'

Perhaps we can put it this way: we can say that Christian faith provides three things which we all desperately need. First, it gives us the assurance, and from time to time the awareness, of a *presence*. This is the presence of God in the world, which can relieve us of the dreadful sense of loneliness, the feeling of 'nothingness' or absence, which so often marks our lives, making us miserable some of the time and insecure all of the time. We reach out for meaning; we find that we are embraced in the arms of a Lover. So Robert Frost, the American poet, once put it. Secondly, it gives a *perspective*, delivering us from a 'worm's eye' view of the world and of our own human existence, as also from our cheap self-centeredness and our easy acquiescence in merely superficial concerns. By this presence and this perspective, life is now seen to have point, purpose, and value; it is redeemed from triviality and frustration and from human cupidity and mean-ness. But above all, we are given a *power*—a power which enables us to live boldly and faithfully and to act with dignity. It 'strengthens us with might by the Spirit in the inner man.'

The power of which we are speaking is the one truly strong

thing in the world, despite all appearances to the contrary. It is not a coercive power, which would push and thrust and shove and manipulate and over-ride; rather, it is the power of genuine love, which is indeed 'the power of God unto salvation to everyone who believes.' That power is astounding in its affects. It can make what is ugly into something truly beautiful; it can make wickedness serve the cause of the genuinely good; it can make dishonesty the agent of abiding truth; it can make our human lovelessness into the wonder of love. That is to say, it is a *redeeming* power. The ancient Christian writer Clement of Alexandria said that it 'turns our sunsets into a sunrise.' A fine hymn by Dean Samuel Crossman of Bristol, found in some of our hymn-books, tells us that it is 'Love to the loveless shown/ that they may lovely be . . .' I like that word 'lovely', for it connotes graciousness, harmony, and the right ordering of life. The power which is God's love-in-act enables us, who are his children, in some degree to learn to 'care', as the Quakers like to style it, to have a concern laid on our hearts, as they also sometimes put it, for other people in their need, by leading us to put our lives alongside theirs and to do all that we can to bring about the full realization of their potentiality as our sisters and brothers.

Thus the fundamental task of a 'churchman' or 'churchwoman' is to celebrate and to proclaim such presence and perspective and power, resulting from God's activity in Jesus Christ. Obviously it is too great a task for any of us to presume to undertake, of and by human effort alone. This is why those who would be sincere disciples of Christ must let the Holy Spirit stir up in them the very things that they would bring to others. The faithful 'church person' needs first of all, then, to open her or his life to an awareness of that presence and perspective and power. Here is the presence of divine Love enfleshed in our midst, in a fellow human being. Here the perspective of Love's purposes, being worked out in the creation, can become our own 'slant' on everything that we experience and know and do. Here also the power which is that same Love, 'shed abroad in our hearts', can give us the strength to witness and to do, above all to 'endure' when the going gets hard and we feel inclined to give up and turn to less exacting activities and interests. For one of the sad things about us is precisely in this fatigue which can lead us to forget our responsibility or to neglect our plain duty, just because we are 'tired Christians' who would prefer to let somebody else, perhaps God himself, do all the work!

For these reasons it is well for us to think much about the faith which the gospel awakens and the life which the gospel empowers. It is necessary to let our minds dwell frequently on the presence of God in all his works, but above all on God's presence in his Son Jesus Christ, finding in the gracious humanity which he wore as a royal garment the vivid imaging of the unseen reality of Love which is in and behind all things. So also it is necessary to let our minds dwell on the vision which comes when we look at him, seeing our little lives in the right (even if for us very humbling) perspective of the divine Charity. It is necessary, too, that we let our minds dwell on the power which *is* that divine Charity; but above all it is necessary to let our hearts be opened to the coming of that power. Surely we can and must do what is within our ability to respond by that opening of heart to the inflowing of the grace which is Love-in-action. The task of every Christian, whether ordained or unordained, is to serve in this and every age as a channel through which the gracious love of God in Jesus Christ may flood the world.

As to the Christian community, the Church, we need to recognize that it is strong, in the only proper meaning of that word, when it is engaged in this great task. When the Church spends its time and energy in its own business, concerning itself primarily with its institutional aspects and agencies (essential as these may be), turned in upon itself in order to preserve at all costs its position and its prerogatives, the Church is weak. Not only so, it is also absurd. And its labors are then those of the fanatic described by George Santayana as one who 'has forgotten his aim in his zeal to redouble his efforts.' Even more than that, a Church which is so introverted is a scandalous denial of its only reason for existence; therefore it is in apostasy from its Lord. That reason for existence is to be God's agency for 'shedding his love abroad in the hearts' of his people. A Victorian minor poet once wrote that the Church's 'watchword' was to be *Amo* ('I love'). He was profoundly right in putting it that way, since the point in and behind Christian activity is or should be nothing but the love which is of God towards his human children and which is meant to be shared by those children.

The dullness, deadness, and dreariness of so much of the 'doing' of the Christian community is a reflection of its forgetfulness of this truth. Yet in the course of a long life, I have yet to know of a parish or congregation, in which parson and people were alert to the faith in something like the way I have tried to present, and acted out that faith in their common life through 'love of the brethren', which could be called dull or dead or dreary. It is stupid to expect people to be attracted to an institution or society which centers itself on itself; nobody in interested in such a group. The Christian Church can only become alive as it moves on in history as a 'pilgrim Church' which is 'in process', focusing its life on God's loving care in Jesus Christ, and finding for itself and for its members the vocation of bringing this reality to the whole world in that world's strange complexity and with all its sad need.

To participate in the Church's ministry is to respond to the call to be under-shepherds of the Good Shepherd. It is to respond as a servant of the servants of God, of *all* God's children wherever they may be. And for those who are ordained, it is not to receive some status or acquire some place of social privilege. Rather, it is to answer the invitation to function for a living fellowship in sharing a common life for others. For all Christians it is to participate in the outgoing of God's love, with the demands which the divine love makes but with the glory that obedience offers.

I have spoken of 'function' a great many times. But I have not suggested that the ministering agent of Christ, ordained or unordained, is to be 'a functionary' in the modern sense of that word. A 'functionary' is usually somebody who possesses status and whose activity is directed *at* others. One who 'functions' acts *for* others. The Good Shepherd, we have been told, came 'to seek and to save', not 'to have and to hold.' He is the model of Christian ministry. He is our Lord and Master; and we who belong to him, as members of his Church, need to remember that 'the servant is not above his Master.'

Celebration

In recent years there has been much talk about 'celebration' as a central concern of the Christian Church. In reaction from concentration on what was known as 'secular Christianity', with its primary stress on Christian interest in the world's affairs, and in an effort to undercut the negative attitude of the so-called 'death of God' school of thought, which focussed on non-religious interests to the exclusion of 'religious' or pietistic devotion, many Christian leaders have moved to an emphasis on the joyous aspect of Christian life and have urged that not only in formal worship but in many other ways we need a recovery of delight in the world as *God's* world and a grateful celebration of what God is and what God has done in that world. An example of this movement may be found in the writings of the American theologian Harvey Cox, whose first book (which had a large circulation) had to do with what he styled 'the secular city', but who later wrote a celebratory study of Christian life; he called this book *The Feast of Fools*. In it he presented the case for a joyful, indeed almost a playful, understanding of Christianity. In that book and in more recent ones too Cox has spoken of his re-discovery of the celebration of life, and of God present and active in life. God's ways in the world are to be greeted with enthusiasm and with acts of worship, both social and personal, that proclaim our joy in him and in what he does in the creation.

Some have dismissed this new emphasis as 'merely faddish.' I cannot agree. But however we may interpret it, I am convinced that one of the important aspects of Christian ministry, both among the generality of believers and with those who have been ordained to a specific function in that ministry, is precisely in such glad celebration. We are to celebrate God's 'mighty acts' (as biblical theologians have put it) in Jesus Christ and in what went before to prepare for him as well as what has resulted from his coming. We are also to celebrate the goodness of life, the beauty of creation, and the way in which (once they have been redeemed from their wrongness) all men and women can reflect something of the glory of God. Such celebration naturally finds expression in the worship which is at the heart of the Christian enterprise. This worship is 'eucharistic', which means that it is thankful and joyful, as the very word 'eucharist' (Greek for thanksgiving) makes clear.

This brings us to the place of sacramental worship, centered in the Holy Eucharist. No longer can Protestant Christians think of worship as consisting of 'preliminaries' before the sermon is preached; no longer can Catholics think of worship as an almost automatic exercise in which the ordained priest performs the rite with others present as passive spectators. *All* are involved in a joyous celebration of God's creative activity and of God's decisive presence in Christ.

In the early days of the Christian Church, its members assembled each Lord's Day to 'break bread'—that is, to observe and take part in the Lord's Supper or Holy Communion. Until the sixteenth century, in all parts of the Christian world the Eucharist (as it came to be called—as we have seen, the word is from the Greek for 'Thanksgiving') was the great act of Christian worship. It began as the celebration of the 'mysteries' of Christ's life, where the faithful gathered themselves together to 'remember' him, following what the first three gospels tell us was his command 'on the night in which he was betrayed', as St. Paul also says in I Corinthians. This act of worship included both the sacramental rite itself and also preaching or proclamation. In the latter the Lord was proclaimed, as in the former he was 'received by faith with thanksgiving.' The great Reformer Martin Luther put this point by saying that the Word which is preached in the sermon is the same Word which is received in the sacrament.

Luther intended that this practice of sacrament and preaching, put together in one 'service', should continue as the norm for Sunday worship. So did John Calvin, the Genevan Reformer who was the founding father of the 'Reformed' communions. So also was the intention of Zwingli, whose desired form of worship was a quite simple observance of the Lord's Supper with the proclamation of the gospel as an integral part of it. The English Reformers, responsible for *The Book of Common Prayer* of the Church of England and her sister churches, likewise meant the Eucharist to be central—as the place to which it was assigned in the bound Prayer Book clearly indicates. Alas, for many reasons, the Genevan civil rulers were not 'up to' Calvin's desire; and more generally, and for what might be styled 'sociological reasons', this centrality was not maintained in most non-Catholic communions. In Scotland there was an exaggerated fear that too frequent communion would make the service seem a mere routine and therefore the Lord's Supper came to be celebrated only quarterly. Thus the wish of the great Reformers, which was identical with the ancient practice of the Church Catholic, was not generally carried out. This is why we have a situation which to an early Christian would have seemed extraordinary; in many places there is a service with preaching as the chief event and the focus of interest, with 'early morning' (in Anglican circles) and very occasional celebrations (in other groups) as the accepted thing.

Within the past half-century, however, the Reformed and Lutheran churches have slowly but surely been returning to the ancient practice. Of course this return is not universal and has often been resisted; even today it is not always accepted by members of these churches as the normal and proper, as it is also the specifically Christian, practice. One still finds that a non-sacramental service is widely supported; and yet to anybody who knows Christian history, the Lord's Supper is the proper mode of Sunday worship. It is interesting to note here that one denomination, founded in the United States during the early years of the last century, has been zealous in re-establishing the Lord's Supper as the normal act of worship week by week. I am referring here to the so-called 'Disciples of Christ', in one of whose theological schools I had the opportunity, a few years ago, to serve as a visiting professor for one academic term. This denomination has a million or more members; numerically it cannot rival the major American Christian groups; but it has witnessed to all such groups in that and the historical centrality of the Eucharist. Anyone who is sensitive to the ways things are going, in most if not all Protestant and Reformed churches, will testify that once again the Holy Communion is coming to be recognized for what it is, although (as I have said earlier) some congregations are not yet prepared to act in practice upon what in principle they accept.

The celebration of what God has done in Christ, rejoicing in his work of redemption and 'doing' what he commanded to be done 'in remembrance' of him: here is a chief function found in the exercise of a functional ministry in the Christian Church. For this reason, if for no other, the *ordained* minister ought to see himself chiefly as acting as the leader or 'president' (as some contemporary liturgies phrase it) in this celebration. The *unordained* person must see his or her role as participant in that celebration, by regularity of attendance and faithfulness in receiving the sacrament. Thus the unordained also have their proper ministry; indeed we may say that it is *they*—the Church gathered in one place and at one time, week by week—who are the celebrants of the Eucharist, although necessarily some one person (the ordained minister) acts on their behalf. In so doing, that ordained person acts for the Body of Christ which is the Church, in its universal or 'catholic' existence; and the ordained person also acts for Christ *in* that Body, since, as the Epistle to the Ephesians makes clear to us, Christ and his Body are indissolubly one.

I have put this first in our consideration of the functioning ministry because the Lord's Supper is the vivid summary of the whole range of Christian faith and life, once we have penetrated beneath the words and have come to understand what is signified in the action. St. Thomas Aquinas once said that 'in this sacrament the whole of our salvation is gathered up.' And it is gathered up in an *action*. Jesus did not command his disciples to think about him or to say things about him; he told them that they were to '*do* this' in his remembrance.

Something which is *done* . . . and so we now turn to consider what takes place when this 'doing' occurs. We are told in the New Testament that Jesus 'in the night in which he was betrayed, took bread, and when he had given thanks he broke it, and gave it to his disciples, saying "Take, eat, this is my body which is given for you." Likewise after supper he took the cup, and when he had given thanks, he gave it to them, saying "Drink this all of you, for this is my blood of the new testament, which is shed for you and for many. Do this as oft as you shall drink it, in remembrance of me." '

What Jesus did at that Last Supper the Christian Church has continued to do over the centuries. The whole is an action, as I have said. There is a taking, a thanking over, in the case of the bread a breaking, and then a giving to those who are participant. The action is set in a total context of worship in which the Christian fellowship gathers to 'make Eucharist'—to give thanks to God and to celebrate the reality of new life in Jesus Christ.

The 'operational words', as modern logicians would call them, are: *take, give thanks* (or bless), *break,* and *give.* Jesus at the Last Supper *took* bread and wine which had been provided for the meal. He *gave thanks* to God according to the traditional Jewish custom of blessing through thanking. He *broke* the bread, so that it might be shared with others present. Then he *gave,* first the bread and later the cup of which all were to drink. In the gathering of the disciples with him, there was thus a communal sharing in what he was soon to do, to suffer, and to accomplish. This is what might well be styled the fourfold pattern of eucharistic action. When the Church today observes the Lord's Supper, it repeats that fourfold action, by which Jesus binds to himself those who were and are to be his people, his heralds, his messengers, his ministers, in a communion of love whose result is to make all who participate 'other Christs' to their brothers and sisters because they now 'dwell in him and he in them.' To become 'other Christs': the phrase was used by St. Benedict in the fifth century and again used by Martin Luther in the sixteenth century. Each of them meant that every Christian is by definition to be *alter Christus,* an 'other Christ', who both represents and acts for the Lord because each Christian belongs to, and is a 'member' of, that one Lord.

I now wish to suggest that the four parts of the eucharistic action provide a clue to the whole meaning of our Christian profession. Things are done; and what is done is an indication of what Christian existence is always to be and what Christian people are always to be doing. For all who share in the broken bread and in the cup are by that means made one with their Lord and with one another. St. Augustine described this when he spoke of 'the mystery of ourselves' at the holy table. A modern writer has put it when he speaks in this fashion: 'We who are already the Body of Christ receive the Body of Christ so that we may more and more become the Body of Christ.' The point here is the identification of human life with the life of God in the manhood of Christ; with this is necessarily associated the way in which the communicant is increasingly brought into closer union with his Lord. And that carries with it the implication that the communicant is also one with his 'even-Christians', those who share in the life of Christ, whose task is so to live and so to act, that this human fellowship is seen as more than a merely human enterprise; it is a deep relationship of mutual love with others, whether they acknowledge Christ or whether they do not recognize the one in whom the divine Love is brought near.

In this consideration of what goes on in the Eucharist, I am not concerned with the question of the *how* of our Lord's presentness there. There have been many theories about this. Indeed, I do not much like the common use of the word 'presence' and I have used in the preceding sentence another, 'presentness.' My reason for this is that it can deliver us from such theoretical issues and enable us to put the stress on the experiential fact that, however this may be accomplished, Jesus makes himself available to and known by his people as they gather together, receive the bread and wine, and celebrate what he has accomplished and what he has won for them. The *how* is a mystery, like all the deep and wonderful things in human experience, such as love shared between human beings. Instead of spending time on the unanswerable question of *how,* it is surely wiser and more reverent to use some words of Richard Hooker, the sixteenth century divine, who wrote about the sacrament, 'O my God, thou art true; O my soul, thou art happy!' If we concentrate on the *that,* not on the *how,* we have come close to the joy experienced in the Lord's presentness. If we worry too much about the *how,* we are quite likely to find that the wonder has vanished. We have tried to 'lay it on the line', as it were; and the result may be that the glory of the experience vanishes in the speculation in which we engage. Something like this is true of the reality of human love, to which I have just referred. If I spend time in an effort to analyze precisely how and why my friend and I love one another, the sheer joy of our relationship may very probably be dissolved. It is much better simply to accept the fact and to delight in it.

Yet we must ask what happens in the Lord's Supper. Obviously we are brought into deep communion with the Lord. But also, if perhaps less obviously, we are privileged to be caught up into his life and share in his offering of himself to the Father. That offering was brought to its climactic conclusion on Calvary, but it also marked the entire period of his earthly obedience to the Father's will. *Tota vita Christi mysterium sacrificium,* said a medieval writer: 'The entire life of Christ is the mystery of sacrifice'. It came to its supreme moment when the Lord gave himself on the Cross. To that offering God responded, in 'raising him from among the dead.' Love like that, given to the limit, could not 'be holden of death.' Of course you and I cannot offer Christ to the Father; but *he,* with whom in communion we are united in deepest mutual indwelling, can and does offer *us* with him to the Father. He takes our poor willing, our meager loving, and even our sinful living once repented of; and he brings us to his and our Father, along with himself, as 'a reasonable, holy, and lively sacrifice.'

But let us return, after this brief excursus, to the four parts of the eucharistic action. First, as to the 'taking.' Christ the Good Shepherd, took life—all life, above all the life of humankind, as it is lived by ordinary men and women. Thus taking it, he related directly to himself, he made it his own. And then, having 'taken life', he 'gave thanks for it.' That is the second point. By linking life with the working of God and with all human rejoicing in God and in God's creative purpose (which includes all that is and all that happens, save for evil and sin and wrongness), Jesus identified his own doing with the perfect will of the Father. In the third place, he was ready and glad to let life, as symbolized by bread, be broken. Indeed he 'broke' his own life, in that he allowed it to be shattered and betrayed, so that the divine Charity might be made more available through that very brokenness of life in which all men and women in very truth share. It was broken for the healing of the world's ills and its restoration to God. Lastly, Jesus gave life to his disciples. He gave them renewed and restored and redeemed life; he gave it to them through the very breaking of it, with the consequence that in him and through him all might share the life which was one with the Father and the love which is inexhaustible and indefatigable—good, right, and true life, now and to all eternity.

The eighteenth century devotional writer William Law, whose writings were much beloved by John Wesley, once said that all Christians are to share in what he styled 'the process of Christ.' What I have just tried to outline *is* that 'process.' The taking or accepting of life as it is and where we are; the relating of it all to God's ongoing purpose of love; the offering of it to the Father; and the giving of it to others: this is the 'process' which in a Christian is repeated. The result is precisely the presence, the perspective, and the power, about which we spoke in the last chapter.

Every time a Christian congregation gathers to celebrate the eucharistic action, with its 'continual remembrance of the sacrifice of the death of Christ and the benefits which we receive thereby', those who assist in the action are caught up into the 'process' and it comes alive in them.

Now we come to the crucial point for the Christian minister, ordained or unordained. For is not the clue to the ministering life of the servants of the servants of God given us just here? The minister is indeed to proclaim the gospel. If the minister is ordained, this will be through sermon and teaching; about that we shall speak in the next chapter. But the very existence of the minister, in its depths and for every Christian, is surely such participation in 'the process of Christ.' The ordained minister leads in or presides at the celebration of that process. And if the Church's reality is in that sharing; if every member of the Church is also caught up into that reality; then in a very particular and vivid sense the Eucharist is the visible and vital manifestation of Christ's life of taking, blessing, breaking and giving. Our Christian vocation to act for the Lord in whom we have our 'wholeness' or salvation is empowered and strengthened by our eucharistic participation. For the ordained minister, to preside at that action is the greatest joy and the most humbling privilege that can be conceived. For *all* of the Christian family, it is a joy and a privilege.

Both the ordained minister and the lay person must as a Christian learn to take life where and as it is found, knowing that in ways past our finite understanding it is all, somehow, 'commanded by God.' That is to say, it is the sphere in which God is active and in which God may therefore be discovered at work. The Christian is then to give thanks for life in all its aspects, relating it to God and to God's loving purpose, finding joy in seeing the place where and the way in which God can be served. The Christian will know broken life, including his or her own, and share with other men and women in their brokenness. For all men and women are *broken,* living broken lives among broken hopes and broken dreams, in broken relationships, and often with broken hearts. To recognize this brokenness is not to succumb to pessimism but to face things realistically, with awareness of the deep tragedy which marks human existence despite its joys and delights. To participate in that brokenness is an enormously painful experience yet it is also an enriching privilege. And finally the Christian is to be one who gives life; for a Christian this is renewed and enriched life, in Christ, which can bring assurance and confidence in God whose will is to give his children hope, peace, joy, and love. The needy and sometimes desperate men and women of our age, in particular, must have such a steadying of life; and it is the Christian ministry to function to provide just that steadying

If this is true, both the ordained and the unordained minister must be a 'eucharistic person.' By this I mean that he or she must be what St. Ignatius of Antioch meant when years ago he spoke of Christ's people as 'living eucharists'—living persons whose existence is in the celebration of God and his redemptive activity for us. In another book, called *Life as Eucharist* (Eerdmans, 1973) I once wrote about the several ways in which something of this thanksgiving is necessarily true of every devout and humble Christian. Here I should stress that in respect to the ministering of the Christian to others this is above all a requirement. Also, I should urge that the ordained person, above all, is to become a dedicated ministering agent of Christ. Every Christian is called to be 'a living sacrifice' to God, offering self totally to the service of the heavenly Father; the ordained person is signally to be seen as just such a 'living sacrifice.'

A little thought about these matters will make it plain that such a picture rules out, once and for all, any and every individual claim, all personal pride, every desire for status and position. For the ordained minister, the terrible danger can come when all too human pretensions are allowed to edge their way into that person's mind. Of course the minister has been ordained as leader and guide. Yet such as one can never forget what the old Scots divines loved to call 'the crown rights of Jesus Christ.' Nor can the ordained person forget that the crown which Jesus wore was a crown of thorns. The Lord's life was marked at every point by sacrifice and service, to the point of giving even unto death in the interests of others. Thoughts like these will also help the non-ordained to have the right notion of what their pastor and priest is about, what he is there for, and how they may properly regard and esteem that leader and assist in the correct understanding of the office and ministry which is proper to ordination. It is not through personal merit or gifts possessed by accident of birth or inheritance or education, that the ordained person has been called to preside at the Lord's Supper. The celebration of the Eucharist—those 'holy mysteries which [the Lord] instituted and ordained . . . as pledges of his love, and for a continual remembrance of his death, to our great and endless comfort'—as the grand words of the old Anglican Ordinal put it—requires the ordained minister, as well as each of the people for whom he ministers as president of the service, to 'search and examine [his or her] conscience, and that not lightly, and after the manner of dissemblers with god,' so that people 'may come holy and clean to such a Heavenly Feast, in the marriage-garments required by God in holy Scripture, and be received as worthy partakers of that holy Table.' So the Ordinal continues; and it is just this that we should take to heart.

To recognize, to accept, and to live out the taking, the offering of thanks, the breaking, and the giving of life, as Jesus did in the days of his flesh in Palestine, is the exacting demand laid upon every Christian and *a fortiori* upon every ordained minister in the fellowship called by the name of Jesus Christ. To celebrate this, with joy and thanksgiving, and thus to play one's small part in making 'heaven's eternal arches ring, with his beloved name' (as the hymn says), is an amazing privilege, not in any way confined to those ordained to preside; yet at the same time it is particularly theirs as being precisely such leaders.

Several times I have quoted the superb English phrases from the old Anglican Ordinals, parallels to which may be found in the ordination services of other Christian bodies. There are some other words in the Anglican Ordinal, which express the purpose of that ministering: that 'as well by the ministers as by them over whom they shall be appointed thy ministers, thy holy Name may be for ever glorified, and thy blessed kingdom enlarged.' This is indeed nobly phrased. We might wish that some of it had been put in a different way. The language is archaic, to be sure, but that is not so difficult for us as the way in which it appears to make a sharp contrast between 'thy ministers' and 'them over whom . . . .' The trouble is in that phrase, 'over whom'; surely in authentic Christian understanding there can be no such 'grading' of rank. We have but one Lord; all the rest of us, clergy or laity, are servants. We should prefer to say, I think, not 'over whom', but 'for whom and with whom.' If the New Testament is to be trusted, that is what we ought to say. Again, when we read of glorifying God's 'holy name' and of the 'enlarging' of God's kingdom, we need to be quite clear as to our meaning. Taught as we are that the gospel is essentially the affirmation of God's saving love in action—or better, the affirmation of God in action in his saving love—we should wish to see the 'glorifying of God's holy name' as primarily the recognition and celebration of his exceeding great love toward us, which carries with it the corollary that we are to be urgent in our desire to work with our human brethren in establishing new dimensions and new occasions where that cosmic Love may be adequately manifested in the affairs of this world, in justice and in peace. 'And God's blessed kingdom' is not only the sovereign rule of God in the world of humans and of nature, although that is part of the truth. It is *also,* if the gospel is accepted, the free response of those people, and in the whole of nature, to that same cosmic Love.

Yet we do not deny the intention of those ancient words from the Ordinal. On the contrary, we wish only to expand their meaning by taking advantage of the results of long years of devoted biblical study by scholars. For along with that work there has been deeper insight into the dynamic structure of the universe, an awareness which we owe to science and associated disciplines. When we put these two together, we may be prepared to grasp the astounding truth that the living God is ceaselessly at work in a changing world; and that the living God who is thus at work is also, and first of all, the loving God who is self-identified with the creation and who seeks always for a responsive movement from the creation. This God is concerned to save his children from their stupidity and cupidity, from their frustration and triviality, and thus to bring them to himself so that they may become genuinely and fully human. The consequences of this newer knowledge can have tremendous implications for our eucharistic celebration.

No longer can we set that action apart from the world of human experience, of historical development, of existential situation, and of natural order. Far too often, in the history of the Church, this sort of separation has taken place. Then the Eucharist has become an esoteric rite in which an elite may share; it is for the pious few. To think and act in that fashion is to deny the wonderful breadth, depth, and height of the Eucharist. For the Lord's Supper is the plain placarding before our eyes, and before the world, of the total reality of God's loving activity towards us and with us and in us. Here material things—bread and wine, with all that has gone into their making—are used; hence the material world is recognized as being *God's* world. What is more, in this eucharistic action, human agents follow Christ's command and the Lord comes in love to his human children. Hence the human sphere is known as the place of God's self-disclosure. Here the bread and wine, received by faithful men and women, are the means by which the presentness of that Lord is given to his people. Hence we see that God can and does take creaturely things and persons and inform them with his very self.

Those who are present at the eucharistic celebration share together in a great ministerial act. The ordained minister is 'celebrant'; but he celebrates on behalf of and with the 'People of God.' All rejoice in God's goodness, his purpose, his love, his redemptive work for his children. To have a part in that act of worship is indeed to proclaim, with enormous joy, the wonder of God's love; it is central to the Christian enterprise. To be a Christian *is* to be a eucharistic person, in whose daily life thanksgiving is the dominant motif and service for others the necessary consequence.

Preaching and Teaching

We must never forget that one of the essential aspects of the Church's ministry is the proclamation of the gospel or, in the phrase often used at the time of the Reformation in the sixteenth century, 'the preaching of the Word.' In the last chapter I sought to set the proclamation in the wider context of celebration. I also said that the ordained minister is especially appointed to lead the people of God in their joy and thanksgiving as they celebrate what God has done in Jesus Christ. But there are two considerations which must also be added. First, the fact that proclamation is normally in the context of celebration does not in any way minimize the importance of the former, any more than it denies the additional task in ministering which has to do (as the title of this chapter suggests) with teaching about Christian faith and life; and second, every member of the Church, including the unordained men and women who constitute the greater number of Christian people, also has a part in proclamation, even if this is not usually by 'preaching' in the sense of 'delivering sermons.'

It is unfortunate that in many circles, however, the ministering function is often put in an entirely separate category and an ordained minister is called 'a preacher', as if this exhausted his responsibilities and privileges as a leader of God's people in their Christian life. Proclamation is always to be seen in the wider context, which includes celebration and also shepherding and witnessing, as we shall see.

From the most cursory survey of the history of the Christian community it is apparent that the proclamation of the gospel, both inside the church-building at services of worship and outside that building in a great variety of ways, has always been an integral part of ministerial responsibility. Christian faith is centered in the *Word,* or 'the Self-Expressive Activity' of God, focussed in the event of Jesus Christ and its consequences. Inevitably that Word must be put into *words,* or human speaking, if it is to be communicated. Recent biblical study, in this instance largely under the impulse generated by Professor C. H. Dodd, has made much of this; it has spoken of the *kerygma* or 'heralding' of the gospel. Paul, for example, wrote often about this *kerygma,* for which he believed he had been called by God on the Damascus Road when he was 'met' by the risen Lord Jesus Christ.

In the earliest days, this proclamation was of course largely outside the regular meetings of the community for worship. Its purpose was to win others for the fellowship. Later much of the proclamation took place within the services of worship; and at that time it became a responsibility laid largely, if not entirely, on those who had been ordained to leadership. In other words, it was regarded as a part of the function proper to one who had been called, chosen, and ordained. The role of the unordained, in this connection, was minimized or neglected.

So also with much of the teaching or (in the New Testament word) *didache.* Teaching is not identical with proclamation but it is closely associated with it. Teaching in earliest days meant the preparation of catechumens, men and women soon to receive baptism; this was done by the presentation of the doctrinal implications of, as well as the moral requirements attaching to membership in the Christian Church. The distinction between the two was probably not quite so sharp as Dr. Dodd argued; obviously the two often overlap and affect one another. But there was, and there is, a distinction between them. Anybody can see the difference between proclaiming what God has done for his human children in Jesus Christ, on the one hand, and the implications—in many areas of life and experience—of that doing of God, on the other. The usual understanding through Christian history has been that it is primarily to the ordained minister that both of these duties are assigned. Incidently, in Scotland there is the interesting use of the word 'dominie' (master or teacher) for the parish minister and also for the school-teacher. But it ought to be clear today that the non-ordained person also has responsibility for teaching others about the implications of Christian faith, just as he or she has a responsibility for announcing to others the wonderful fact that in Christ God has indeed acted.

Let us now turn to the preaching aspect of the ministerial function, focusing more especially on the work of the ordained minister although with suggestions and implications which apply also to the lay person within the Christian fellowship. Then we can turn to the teaching which has been so much a part of the ongoing life of that fellowship.

I have emphasized the way in which sacrament and proclamation have commonly been considered as constituting the regular act of worship of the Church; the two have belonged together. The proclamation gives its interpretation to the sacrament; the sacrament establishes the presentness of the Lord about whom the proclamation has been made. Thus we can say that in his functional responsibility the ordained minister—the priest, pastor, leader, president—is called both to proclaim God's Word *and* to celebrate that Word in sacramental leadership. I wish to make four points about the task of proclamation.

The first point is insistence that 'preaching' is to be nothing other than *proclamation of the gospel.* This tells us that there is no ministerial commission to talk about the 'values' of religion generally conceived, nor about the superiority of theism to other possible philosophies, nor about morality whether traditional or contemporary; neither is there a commission to defend the established 'ways of life' which in this or that society are taken to be important or desirable or necessary. During the many years that I taught in a theological school in the United States I found it necessary again and again to warn my students, who were soon to be ordained ministers, against what was then a common practice in many congregations: the preaching of sermons which in fact were only lectures on the 'American way of life.' Now that I am again in England, the same sort of warning has often seemed needed: Sermons on the British way of life are often enough delivered; they are nothing other than an exaltation, in what amounts to a patriotic lecture, of the attitudes and outlook which are prevalent in this land. Happily, on both sides of the Atlantic there is now a recognition of the error of this substitute for the proclamation of the gospel. Hence there is much less danger of a perversion in which the doubtless good and valuable national modes of life, either in the United States or in Britain, will be presented as if they were central to the gospel. The Church's ordained and unordained members have been given the one task of proclaiming that gospel, which is about God in terms of Jesus Christ, crucified and risen. Anything else may be useful or helpful, but there is no place for it in the pulpit of the Christian Church.

It is equally important to point out that the sermon is not a theological lecture. The preaching is to be theologically informed, to be sure; but that is different from turning it into a discourse on some theological topic. It is true that anyone who ventures to proclaim the gospel must be aware of what theology has to say; after all, we humans are rational beings who ought to be ready to use our brains! That is different from turning a church-service into an occasion for the discussion of theology, whether traditional or radical. A sermon is theological in that it is always a 'word about God'; it is not theological if that means learned discourse more suitable for a theological college or the department of theology in a university.

The proclamation or preaching of the gospel has to do with inviting men and women to respond in faith to God's act towards humankind. It also has to do with the way in which 'the faith' (the Church's agreed understanding of what the response of faith requires) has come to be. But it is easy to substitute here what used to be called 'definite Church teaching', as if this in itself constitutes the gospel of God in Christ; it is also easy to substitute one's own speculative interpretation for that gospel. Neither of these is genuine proclamation. Nor is moral exhortation or the 'giving of good advice.' Good advice may well be important, if it comes from those who know what they are talking about. Moral exhortation is often required, more particularly if some people fail to realize that a specific kind of living—living 'in Christ' and as Christ's ministering agent—is a necessary consequence of the response in faith to what God has done for us. But these are not in themselves the content of the *kerygma*. The gospel has to do with what might well be called the *divine indicative*; moral *imperatives*, or any other kind of imperative, should be seen as the consequence of that indicative. The basic concern in proclamation is what God has done, is doing, and will do, as we apprehend this through the event we name when we speak of Jesus Christ.

The result of the preaching of the gospel, we may devoutly trust and hope, will be a Christian moral life, both in matters personal and in matters social. There are indeed tremendous implications of the gospel for what we ought to do, how we ought to live, and how we ought to conduct our affairs. These are never to be forgotten nor minimized; but I repeat that the place to point to them, discuss them, and try to develop them and their consequences in concrete behaviour, is not the regular Sunday sermon.

What I have been saying in the last few paragraphs implies that all preaching has also a prophetic—a proclamatory—quality. Despite a common misunderstanding, a prophet is not usually ordained. The great Jewish prophets, with but one exception (Isaiah) were lay people. They were called not to give good advice; neither were they expected to 'foretell' the future. They were the great proclaimers of God and of God's revealed will. They 'forth-told' rather than 'foretold.' Every Christian ought to have this prophetic quality, although he or she is not necessarily to be ordained— and in any event, nobody *could* be ordained a prophet, since one is called by God as and how God purposes and wills. I shall return to the prophetic aspect of ministry. Here I would only insist that this quality does not preclude, but rather demands, that it be the gospel, the Word of God, which is proclaimed.

When the preaching is set in the context of the Church's worship as celebration, we can see at once how right and natural it is for it to be about the gospel and nothing else. Yet there are other occasions when proclamation is the Christian's responsibility. The work of evangelists, missioners, and the believer's readiness to witness and testify, are relevant here. Only in this fashion can those who are outside the Christian community be brought to hear the Word of God affirmed and declared through the words of men and women and in consequence, as we hope and pray, be won to membership in the community. Nor need this be always in terms of verbal utterance; often enough, the silent witness of faithful life will serve the same purpose. On the other hand, for men and women who already belong and are attendants at the worship of the Church, the need is for the regular and faithful communication of the gospel, so that they are confronted again and again with its reality and with its demand. And it is often the case that somebody may 'drop in' at a service of worship, for one reason or another; she or he should then be presented with the gospel which will be heard in the context of the Church's act of celebration. For such persons the vivid presentation of the *why* of it all is important. That, of course, is what preaching of the gospel provides.

In the second place, I urge that genuine proclamation must be *simple*. I am not for a moment saying that it should be simplistic, childish, or undemanding. While the gospel is understandable by a child, it is not 'childish.' Every preacher must strive for the simplicity, clarity of expression, and straightforward and direct utterance which will convey meaning to the hearers. The people who do hear, as well as those who preach whether they be ordained for this function or lay witnesses to the gospel, are really simple people, even if (perhaps especially if) they consider themselves to be 'sophisticated moderns.' They can best be grasped by what is being proclaimed if that is told to them in language which its understandable and with continuing reference to their own human needs and desires. Jesus himself spoke in this simple way, if the gospel narratives are to be believed, with the use of common analogies and stories drawn from the common life. He was not afraid to use ordinary human experience and the facts of daily life as a way of communicating the reality of God, of God's loving action, and of God's abiding intention for men and women.

To take an obvious example, if people are to realize that God *is* love and that God's *acts lovingly,* there is a ready analogy in the experience of love known to men and women in their human existence here and now. Of course human loving is defective and distorted; yet no preacher need be hesitant about using it as a clue to the divine love. St. Augustine once said that those who know human love can begin to understand something about divine love. Thus we should not accept the sheer disjunction between divine love and human loving which is advocated by Anders Nygren (and others) in books like Nygren's *Agape and Eros.* The real distinction between the two does not amount to an utter contradiction between them. That idea is contrary to biblical evidence, especially in the New Testament; it is psychologically impossible and practically ridiculous. If Jesus was prepared to speak in terms of the human loving known to his hearers as indicative of the divine love of God, why should those who speak on his behalf be afraid to do the same?

In my student days a great teacher used to tell us that an unfailing test of anybody's apprehension of some important subject was to be found in that person's ability to do what he styled 'talk about it fairly simply.' The same applies to the person who proclaims God's act in Jesus Christ. This is why the greatest preachers in the Christian Church yesterday and today have been and are those who know how to speak directly, simply, and in a straightforward manner. They may have spoken out of a great depth of learning and a wide range of experience; but because they really *knew* what they are talking about they were able to see the big points and to stress them in a relatively simple fashion. This may be accomplished in a variety of ways; but an important one is to 'blue-pencil', in any proposed preaching, whatever is too recondite or obscure. This will ensure that the sermon when preached will have the strength and vigour which come from just such simplicity and directness. Too complicated and complex preaching is usually a sign of inadequate preparation; effective preaching comes from striving for the clear and compelling phrase and illustration.

My third point has to do with *relevance*. The gospel of God in Christ is not up in the air; it is very much down to earth. It speaks to men and women where they are and as they are. If the proclamation of that gospel does not do the same, it is very likely not a heralding of what God has done, does do, and will be doing; it will be an exercise in human speculation or a mere theorizing. Perhaps this is why a visiting preacher, however brilliant and eloquent, can never quite get at the congregation which is being visited. If one does not know the people to whom one is preaching, if one is not aware of their needs, then one is not likely to preach so that the words of men, conveying the Word of God, come home to them in anything like the way in which a less eloquent or billiant, yet directly relevant preaching, can do. The person who proclaims God in Christ ought to know those to whom the address is made, to be aware of their situations, to care for them, and thus 'to apply the gospel' (as the old-fashioned phrase has it) to them where they are and as they are.

Of course relevance is not a tailoring of the gospel to the fancies of men and women. What God is up to, what God has done and is doing, are *there*. They must be grasped as being just that. Yet this does not imply that the proclamation is made *in vacuo*, so to speak, without regard for where and how it is heard and understood. An old friend of mine told me that during the week before his Sunday sermon—he was an ordained priest of great learning and sophistication—he would go into the church for half an hour or so. He would seat himself for a minute or two in one place after another; and as he did this, he would say to himself, 'Here

Mrs. Smith sits, here Mr. Jones, here young Adams, here Susan Brown. . . .' As he sat in those places, with these people in mind, he would ask himself what was the concrete situation, what were the deep needs, the urgent desires, the several different problems, which would be present in the minds and hearts of each of those persons. He would ask himself how he could best proclaim God's saving, healing, and helping concern to each one of them, how he could help them grow in faith and in loyal discipleship to the One proclaimed. Then he would prepare his sermon with those people *in mind,* so that on the Sunday he could preach to them *in person.* It was no wonder that this particular parson was so effective in communicating the gospel to the members of his parish; it came as no surprise to us who knew him that he was esteemed as an ordained minister of Jesus Christ who had both compassion and understanding for the people whom he had been called to lead in their Christian profession.

In the fourth place, I suggest that the proclamation of the gospel should never be allowed *to become stale.* If there could be anything worse than a stale sermon, it would be a stale gospel. But the gospel is never stale; and nobody, ordained or unordained, who proclaims it to others should let it seem dull, conventional, uninteresting, and tedious. The gospel is always interesting and exciting. It is interesting because it has to do with God's own interest in his children; it is exciting because it stimulates a zealous and eager response. It is the duty of the person who proclaims it to let this be seen. Sometimes a sermon seems banal because the one who proclaims it has not grasped that interest and excitement. If that is the case, then it is incumbent upon the preacher to consider his own grasp of the gospel and to see whether it has become in his case, or in hers, a matter of little or no importance.

The preaching of the gospel will tend to be stale and dull if the preacher is not alert. It will also be stale and dull if the preacher has no genuine intellectual awareness of what the gospel is concerned to affirm. What is more, it will be dull and stale if the preacher is not spiritually alive. In the next chapter we shall consider the Christian as a scholar, so far as this may be possible. There is nothing to be said for sheer intellectual incompetence, least of all when the person in question is ordained. In a later chapter we shall speak also of the development of a genuine spiritual awareness; for once again there is nothing to be said for spiritual inertia or impercipience, above all in the case of the ordained person whose job it is to lead, and thus help, people to grow in grace as they respond to God's saving activity in Jesus Christ. Just now, I wish to say something about what may be a help to the person whose duty is preaching—and I am talking about what I may call the need for a continual re-conception of the Word proclaimed. Perhaps that will suffice for our present discussion.

A way of avoiding staleness, then, is to engage in just that task of re–conception. In preparing for preaching, the one to whom this duty is given might consider whether the traditional language, learned in the past, will in fact be understandable to those who hear. That language is hallowed by long usage; it has its value in relating us to the tradition in which by baptism we were admitted and in which we now stand. It is not to be thrown out as if it had no significance. Yet it does not always 'get across', because nowadays men and women are not so familiar as once they were with the traditional idiom of Christian speech. This is not their fault; in most cases it results from their not knowing the Bible, not having been admitted to the story of the historical development of religious discourse, not having been trained in their early days in the meaning of the great Christian tradition. The task today is to learn how to put 'in other words' what that traditional language has been attempting to convey. Those 'other words' will be more directly contemporary and therefore more easily comprehended. If they are contemporary and comprehensible, they are likely to be more immediately appealing. We can ask, for instance: 'what is the *real* meaning of "atonement" and how can we find phrases which will retain that meaning and yet say something which is not merely "conventional talk"?' If we do this, we may find language which is fresh in quality and which will speak to those who hear in a fashion that is perhaps unexpected but telling in that very unexpectedness. Secondly, in proclamation it is not so much the quantity as the quality of belief which is significant. Erasmus once spoke a fine word: 'The things which must be believed are to be as few as necessary.' Those things must be believed deeply and genuinely, however. So also the famous King's Book, published in England during the Reformation period, distinguished between what it called 'things necessary' and 'things indifferent.' Thus we need to consider what *is* necessary or essential, what is in fact integral to the gospel, and what is, so to say, 'peripheral'; and we must put our stress on the former and not on the latter. I believe that these two suggestions can help us to maintain the freshness and the relevance of the gospel, so that it may come freshly and relevantly to those who hear.

What has just been said may seem more applicable to the ordained person than to those who are not ordained. It is; yet I urge that every Christian, in his ministry as representative of Christ in his Body the Church, has a responsibility to speak about his faith, when and as opportunity is given, in a way that is simple, relevant, and fresh; and that above all such an one must be sure that it *is* the Christian proclamation that is communicated, rather than something else, and that the proclamation is not cluttered up with side issues and peripheral matters.

Let us turn now to the Christian as a teacher. I have already urged that the two belong together; I now also urge that this teaching responsibility, while in a particular way belonging to those who are ordained, has its wider application for each man or woman who would be a faithful representative of the Lord.

There was a day, now long past, when a parish clergyman would meet with the people from time to time to engage in 'catechism.' This was usually a fairly simple question-and-answer method of instruction, which no longer has much appeal and perhaps little value. But even in those 'old days' a good catechist was not content simply to ask questions and receive the proper answers as they were found in some book or tractate. The catechist would usually explain, illustrate, develop, and apply the material, so that both questions and answers had meaning for those present at the session. Today the Church School, Sunday School, Adult Instruction Class, discussion groups, and the like are more likely to be the scene for such instruction. A former colleague of mine once remarked, in this connection, that in his view every parish and congregation should be 'a school of religious instruction and of teaching about prayer'; however this was to be done, he said, it was a vital necessity in our day. I am sure that he was right in what he said.

Any kind of instruction, under whatever circumstances, should be marked by the qualities which I have already mentioned in relation to preaching. Teaching should be as simple as possible and so far as the subject will permit; it should be relevant, springing from and referred back to the concrete situations in which the learners find themselves; it should be fresh and lively. Most of all, it should be thoroughly Christian, since its chief objective (in our present connection) is to help men and women come better to understand the wider implications of faith in God as self-expressed in Jesus Christ and, in the light of that understanding, to grasp the necessary ways of applying that faith to daily living.

Times of instruction offer an opportunity to present the theological, biblical, devotional, moral, and 'relational' material which does not have a proper place in the proclamation of the Word. In particular, laymen and laywomen can be given the information they need about the development of the Christian tradition and the way in which the theologies which have appeared during the Church's history have sought to interpret the event of Jesus Christ. In this and other ways, they can be encouraged to do their own reading and study. Whatever may be the subject matter, utter honesty and frankness about problems are required in such teaching. Along with this should come a readiness on the teacher's part to admit his or her ignorance where that does in fact exist. If these things are not found, no teacher will receive nor deserve to receive the attention of those being taught. People are always conscious of their teacher's capacity in his or her work, as well as of his or her prentension to a knowledge which is not really present. People are always conscious also, and hence suspicious, of 'talking through one's hat', such as inevitably manifests itself when a teacher is either incompetent or dishonest or pretentious.

The Church has suffered badly during the past few decades because of its failure to inform lay people about the results of many years of devoted and critical biblical study. They are left with a view of Scripture which is unintelligent and impossible. If Christian teachers had informed the people of the Christian community about such biblical study, to take one example, the shock with which the discovery of the so-called 'Dead Sea Scrolls' and their contents was greeted could have been avoided. When people learned, often through secular journals or documentaries, about this material and hence came to know of the influence of Essene and other cultural and literary ideas upon primitive Christian thinking, they were utterly unprepared for these obvious facts; they did not know what to do about them; some even 'lost their faith' because of this newly-discovered material. Learned scholars, themselves devout Christians, and many clergy-people, knew about this likely influence: But the ordinary church person had not been told. That was stupid and its results were often tragic.

Another important result of sound teaching is the avoidance of unnecessary intellectual scandal. The gospel is indeed a *scandalon*, as St. Paul said. But it is an offense and a scandal to human pride, arrogance, selfishness, and sin, not to genuine human intelligence and awareness. To recognize that the gospel is in the right sense an offense is *not* to say that men and women, in their honest (if often misguided) efforts to understand it and relate it to the world which they know, must reject the knowledge which is available in our own time. Today we understand the world and much that is in it in a fashion different from that which was characteristic of our forefathers in the Christian faith. But if the gospel of Christ is true, it will be patient of restatement in the terms which are today accepted by most men and women. This must be recognized and accepted in any teaching which hopes to be effective.

Finally, I return to what I have called the prophetic quality in the ministerial function of the Church and of Christian people. I have said that prophets, when and as they appear, are called by God to speak a word of challenge and warning; they are usually found among the unordained. If they come from the ordained, as did Isaiah, they are the exception rather than the rule. But there *is* a genuine prophetic quality in every Christian's life or work and hence in that Christian's way of ministering. The prophet speaks on God's behalf, proclaiming for weal or woe the will of God. Nobody can deny the importance of that task. What matters is not one's own ideas but what God has done in history, is doing in our own day, and will do in the future which is as much his as is the past and the present. Most often the prophetic quality will be shown in the honesty with which temporary issues are discussed. In our day, the prophetic side is most likely to appear in recognition and consequent denunciation of the selfishness, arrogance, pretension, and domination shown by those 'who have' and their contempt for or rejection of those who 'have not.' In other words, prophetic words will often have to do with the social dimension of Christian action. They will urge a response in the service of the poor, the underprivileged, the neglected, the outcast.

It will be well to let our minds dwell on the responsibility to preach the gospel, on the requirement to teach honestly as a part of ministering, on the danger of indifference, carelessness, and laziness; and on the necessity for us all, and for the ordained in particular, to speak simply, relevantly, and freshly, yet with utter conviction. Jesus as preacher and teacher is the model here, as everywhere else. 'The common people heard him gladly', we are told. This was because he spoke the 'truth in love', with depth and simplicity, with certitude and clarity. Can those who are called to represent him, whether as ordained or unordained persons, aim at anything less? Dare his under-shepherds, the servants of the common folk who are also God's servants, be content to do a second-rate and shoddy job? Surely our Christian vocation makes it clear that this can never be the case, once we have been grasped by the love of God in Christ.

Study and Learning

One of the great works of English literature is George Herbert's *Priest to the Temple*. The seventeenth century Wiltshire poet and parson is commonly regarded by literary critics as a master of style and an outstanding example of what has come to be known as 'metaphysical poetry.' I mention this man and his famous book because in discussing the work of 'the country parson'—he himself was vicar of Bemerton, near Salisbury, whose parish church is a lovely building still used today (a friend of mine now serves the parish, so I have a certain personal interest in it) and well worth a visit—Herbert insists upon study and learning as the mark of a good ordained minister, more especially the study of Holy Scripture with the assistance of what he calls 'commenters and ancient Fathers.'

What Herbert felt to be requisite for the ordained minister also has its significant place in the Christian discipleship, the more general ministry, of any and every Christian. Once again, I urge, there is no great gulf between the ordained person with his special function in the Church's life and the unordained or (as we commonly and inaccurately say) the 'laypeople.' Many who have written about the ordained ministry have stressed the need for study and learning; not so many have recognized that any man or woman who professes the Christian faith should also, so far as this is at all possible for him or her, seek to be well-informed through as much reading and learning as is available and as opportunity offers.

For the clergyman, it is worth noticing that at one time the ordained ministers of the Church of England were called *stupor mundi*—the 'wonder of the world'—by reason of their intellectual competence or, at the very least, their desire to be instructed and informed. Perhaps the same phrase might be used today, but in the contrary sense: such clergy are often remarkable for their failure to use their minds about the basic concerns of Christian faith, worship, and life. Nor is this true only of clergy of the Church of England. Far too many ordained persons, in all communions, are so busy, so active, so overwhelmed by their work, that they think they have little or no time for study. And what is true of the ordained is even more true of vast numbers of unordained Christians. This is an unfortunate, indeed a tragic, situation, since what amounts to 'thoughtless religion' is hardly likely to be interesting, attractive, or compelling to people outside the Christian Church. The Greek philosopher Socrates remarked that 'an unexamined life is not worth living.' May we not rightly say that an unexamined, unstudied, even an ignorant, membership in the Christian community is worth very little?—although it is true, of course, that entrance into the Kingdom of Heaven is for those who are not necessarily learned in mind but certainly are pure in heart.

The distinguished Roman Catholic Modernist leader, George Tyrrell, wrote biting words about those 'who think that Christianity consists in nothing more than going about doing good, especially in the kind of doing good which involves a great deal of going about.' Activism is essential; but it can be an easy substitute for the acquiring of a thoughtful and intellectually respectable understanding of the basics of faith, the meaning of worship, and the grounds for conduct. I conclude that no self-respecting person, ordained or unordained, could wish to follow the example of a young clergyman who said to me, with evident pride, that he had not opened a serious theological volume since he left his college. Incidently, the sermon which I had heard him preach, shortly before he said this, demonstrated admirably that he was correct in his assertion: It was a superficial, even banal, treatment of one of the great themes of Christian faith; and that young man ought to have been ashamed of himself.

Ordained ministers have usually promised at their ordination that they will be diligent in continuing study. To cite once again some words from the Anglican Ordinal, they have publicly declared that they will be diligent 'in reading the Holy Scriptures, and in such studies as help to the knowledge of the same.' They have been exhorted to 'draw all [their] cares and studies this way', toward the 'reading and learning the Scriptures [and to] weighing them' so that they may know 'the teaching which is taken out of Holy Scriptures.' And while unordained men and women have made no such promises nor been given any such exhortation, surely it is fair to say that as a matter of responsible discipleship and with a view to equally responsible ministering on their part, they ought to be both willing and eager to use their brains, to read and study, and thus to learn as much as they can about the Christian tradition, its faith and its life, and whatever else appertains to informed Christian belonging.

Nor should this duty be confined to the study of the Bible, although that is central. As I shall note later in this chapter, much else should be studied. One need not be a professional scholar whose life is devoted to study or academic pursuits. Some have that particular vocation, to be sure; but *all* are called to be as genuinely learned, as fully informed, as they can manage in the time at their disposal. 'The time at their disposal' for most of them is often *more* available than many appear to allow. I have known ordained ministers who say, 'I simply do not have time nor opportunity for reading and study.' I have known devoted Christian 'laypeople' who say the same. Yet I have observed that such people *do* have time, and such people *do* make opportunity, to read popular books, slick magazines and the daily newspaper.

I spoke above of my young friend who boasted that he had not read a serious theological book for many years. Had that ordained minister not been a person of great charm and genuine Christian conviction (however ill-informed) he would have been an egregious failure as a parson. That he was not a failure was due more to the grace of God than to anything that he had done to keep himself useful. But the sad result of his intellectual vacuity was that he 'reeked of the spur of the moment', so to say; he was full of homiletic clichés and secondhand assertions. I doubt if any of us has the right to expect that God will cover our deficiencies when we ourselves do not make any effort. To assume that God will do so is certainly relying on what Dietrich Bonhoeffer so vividly described as 'cheap grace.' And what is true for the ordained minister is equally true for the unordained man or woman in his or her genuine work of ministering for Christ in his Church—granted, of course, that the busy unordained person is not likely to have what might be styled the 'professional' concern to keep alert and informed.

Let me contrast the young parson of whom I have just spoken with a middle-aged Christian who has not been ordained but who is a devout and active communicant of a parish that I know well. This man is engaged in business and he has enormous demands upon his time and energy. Yet he believes that part of his Christian vocation is precisely to spend part of each weekend in studying some significant theological work. He consults his vicar from time to time, enquiring what he might read in order to keep informed. In his own limited way this man has devoted much time to acquiring knowledge of the history of Christian thought. He began with quite simple material but he is now able to master more advanced books. In his own way, he can speak with considerable authority about some topics that have had his attention, such as the way in which Christian faith in Christ has developed in statement and depth over the centuries. I admire him enormously because, as it seems to me, he has taken with utmost seriousness what I believe is part of every intelligent Christian's responsibility.

One of the unhappy results of failure to do this sort of study is the way in which those who speak on behalf of the Christian Church, whether they are ordained or not, so often are appallingly superficial. To read letters written by such persons to the newspapers is to be horrified at the fashion in which their pathetical little ego is bolstered by cheap and easy denunciations or equally cheap and easy assertions. Very often what we read is not an authentic statement of conviction but a secondhand expression of prejudice, and is ill-informed, ignorant, and lacking in understanding and sympathy. No wonder that many non-Christians have come to think that the characteristic mark of those of us who profess the faith is just such ignorance, failure in understanding and sympathy, and unwillingness to face issues honestly and with complete integrity of mind.

I have noted that the Ordinal lays much stress on Holy Scripture. That is what we should expect, for those Scriptures are our basic source-book and anything that is to be received and believed by Christians must be 'proved by most certain warrant of Holy Scripture', as the Thirty-Nine Articles in the English Prayer Book assert. The word 'prove' here is used, as it always was in Elizabethan times, for 'tested.' This helps us to see that we are not to dig out 'proof-texts', in the modern sense, from our reading of the Bible, as if it were a sort of complete religious and moral dictionary or a theological encyclopedia. We are to use the Bible intelligently, following its great themes, understanding its major motifs, and seeking to discover in what events God has disclosed himself in the Jewish-Christian tradition. This is why the use of 'commenters', as George Herbert put it—'commentaries', in our modern idiom—is invaluable in our study of the Scriptures. Anyone who works on the Bible should have at hand some of the best and most up-to-date commentaries and should consult them regularly. Thus the reader will be delivered from a superstitious attitude toward the *ipsissima verba* of the Bible. Such a reader will be able to see growth, development, and variety in the material that is being studied. As it is the source-book of our Christian tradition, account can be taken of the long preparation for, the emergence in history of, and the significant consequences which followed from, the central event of our faith which is the life, teaching, actions, death and resurrection of Jesus Christ. Studied in that way, the Bible is the record of the formative period of Christian discipleship, with its antecedents and its results; it will also be seen as the normative collection of documents for that discipleship.

Apart from the Bible, there are other areas in which a Christian may acquire some competence. The ordained minister, in particular, should know something about the history of the Church and its impact upon society at large, something about the thinking of great Christians in the past and in the present, something about the new learning which gives a context for Christian thought today. There is no need for expert knowledge, but there is genuine need for an awareness of what Matthew Arnold called 'the best that has been thought and said' during the past and of what is being thought and said in our own day. Acquaintance with this broader culture will enable one to have a better grasp of 'what God is up to in his world', not least as this manifests itself in non-religious ways. Every Christian ought to have a genuine openness and a willingness to learn; and for the clergymen to have such openness and willingness is essential. Much is going on in the world today and what is being said may not be, probably is not, all sound and true; but then it is not likely to be all false, either. What I have been urging may seem overwhelming. How shall anybody find time and opportunity to manage it? But in this period of human history, the Christian witness must be heard; and it will not be heard if those who bear it are not genuinely informed men and women. Let me then go on to make some concrete suggestions and offer a few observations about all this. Perhaps these will be useful to my readers as they attempt to undertake their study and acquire the learning which will more fully equip them for their ministering work, whether that be as ordained to a special 'enabling' role in the Church's life or as thoughtful unordained men and women who wish to set their faith in the widest possible context.

First, I believe that it is desirable to work out a plan of study, allowing enough variety to avoid weariness. One might decide, for example, to apply oneself for a year to a single author or a single theme. Here it would be possible to get to know 'in depth', as the saying goes, the contribution of (say) Teilhard de Chardin, the great French Jesuit priest-mystic-palaeontologist whose writings have been published in the past dozen years or so. Or one might choose a living theologian, like John Macquarrie of Oxford, whose books have the great merit of being written in a straightforward and relatively easy style. Perhaps the giants of the last fifty years—Barth, Tillich, Niebuhr—could be taken up. As to single subjects, their range is enormous. I remember a clergyman who decided to read in the ancient Fathers of the Church. He pursued this for many years, with the result that as he came to retirement age he had mastered, with some degree of competence, the major works of the early ages of the Christian tradition. Suggestions for such study, either of an author or a subject, will often be provided by theological colleges and faculties of religious studies in universities, some of which publish annually carefully prepared reading-lists for their former students and others.

If the Bible is to be studied systematically, it is a good idea to acquire a set of commentaries. For the more academic, there are the famous advanced series about which any theological college can be asked; for the rest of us, there are admirable series like the 'Moffatt' or the 'Interpreters', as well as excellent popular series such as those which Penguin Books produced a few years ago, in cheap format, or the Cambridge or Oxford series, the latter pair covering pretty much the whole Bible. I believe that laypeople will profit from such scriptural study while of course it is required work for the ordained person. The Bible can be read for devotional purposes; presumably most thoughtful and devout Christians do this. But it can also be read with more scholarly considerations in mind—and it may be true, as an old friend of mine used to urge, that the devotional and the scholarly approach should often go together.

Many parish clergymen have told me that they find it profitable, as well as a sort of hobby, to take a single Christian doctrine or teaching as their subject. They begin by looking up the biblical material and then follow its development in Christian history, ending up with whatever has recently been written on the topic. In this way they have come to see both the continuity of Christian thought and the many 'break-throughs' as down the ages new approaches and interpretations have been suggested. For those who are more interested in Christian worship or in Christian moral teaching, a similar line of study may be followed. One particular value of this approach to a single doctrine or topic is that the careful student is delivered from too much reliance on the merely contemporary, while at the same time he or she can come to understand more readily why there have been changes in outlook or statement or expression during the long course of Christian history.

But there may be non-religious subjects that yet have a special significance for any Christian. I may perhaps be personal here. Many years ago I decided that it would be useful for me to know something about modern scientific developments, especially in the physical sciences. Certainly I could not claim any real competence in the subject but I thought that I should be informed about the newer physics, so different from the Newtonian physics in which I (like most of my contemporaries) had been brought up as a schoolboy. So I tried to read about and understand—and it took a good deal of effort to do the latter, I confess—modern quantum and relativity physics. To acquire this knowledge, even in the relatively slight way that was possible for me, had the result of preparing me for changes in world view, so that when I came to read the writings of Whitehead (who had been a mathematical physicist before he turned to philosophy) I was prepared for what I found. His thought relied largely on this new physics, of course, and cannot readily be understood without some awareness of what has been going on in that area for the past hundred years. My concern here was in the first instance not a 'professional one'; yet what I learned has had important professional value because it has shown me that many of the negative criticisms of Whitehead, whose general conceptuality I had found highly sympathetic, are made because the critics have no knowledge of his background in modern science and its outlook.

When I first delivered, as lectures to various Christian groups, the material contained in this book, some of my auditors expressed surprise that I ventured to speak so forcibly on the need for study and learning, when my main topic had to do with the ministering responsibility of ordinary Christians, ordained or unordained. That expression of surprise revealed a strangely and sadly mistaken attitude towards persons who are ministers of Christ. Have we forgotten that Jesus told us to love and serve God 'with all our mind', as well as with heart and soul and strength? Someone remarked of my old colleague, the distinguished New Testament scholar Burton Scott Easton, that he 'went to his study as if he were going to the altar to celebrate the Holy Communion.' Obviously most of us can never hope to be scholars of Easton's calibre; but all of us should remember that the consecrated use of our minds regarding the 'things of God' is part of the work which, as the famous Benedictine motto tells us, is closely related to prayer: *orare et laborare*, 'to pray and to work' are two equally indispensable aspects of all Christian vocation. And nowhere is this so true as when we turn to consider the basic teachings of the Christian tradition in which we stand.

We ought to be aware of the best scholarly work on the Scriptures, for example, even though we cannot become experts on the subject. We ought to know something about the development of Christian belief through the long period from the closing of the New Testament canon to our own day, although we need not seek to become experts in this area. To understand these matters will help us to become more effective witnesses to the abiding faith of the Church; and this is equally the case for laypeople and for ordained people. Likewise we need to know something about the contemporary world, with the new knowledge available in our own day in so many different fields. Only then can we minister to the men and women who in fact live in that world and who must be approached as modern people with all the implications of modernity in mind. This does not imply any identification of the gospel with human learning; its implication is, rather, that the God about whom the gospel speaks is the God of the contemporary world in its secular quite as much as in its religious concerns.

This sort of study and learning, in the degree to which we are capable of undertaking it, will help us to avoid two dangers. The first is a simplistic identification of ancient formula or statements with the truth of God. Here the ultra-conservative can give an entirely mistaken representation of that truth, since he or she seems to forget that it is the *'living* God' who 'does *new* things' (as Isaiah said centuries ago) who is proclaimed in Christian faith. Such excessive conservatism, unwilling to face up to changes of idea and interpretation, is 'fighting the grain of the universe', as Whitehead once said. To say old things in a simplistic fashion is often to say something very different from that which our fathers in the faith intended to assert. The second danger is a thoughtless and unhistorical acceptance of anything new, with the assumption that the new is always right. This is absurd, of course. It implies that we can learn nothing from our ancestors; it forgets that ours is indeed an historic faith and can only be properly interpreted when that long history is known and appreciated, so far as we can manage to do this. I have often thought that some presentations of supposed 'orthodoxy', by the ultra-conservative, are in truth really heretical—like my former student who explained the doctrine of the Incarnation as teaching that 'Jesus is God with a skin on'. He defended this teaching by saying that this 'is what the Church has always affirmed.' On the contrary, his explanation was a classical statement of the Apollinarian heresy, condemned in A.D. 381 at the First Council of Constantinople! And on the other hand, when I have heard a very up-to-date layman say in a discussion-group that for the Christian Jesus is divine in some sense because he is 'the best man who ever lived', I have been equally appalled. In terms of classical Christianity, that statement was at best an instance of modern Ebionism (also condemned in the ancient days of the Church) or at worst such a sad confusion of divinity and humanity that presumably to be a splendid man *is* somehow to be identical with the divine activity in the world. Or again, when someone says that Christianity is really 'the teaching of Jesus and nothing more', one is astonished that such a naive idea could be entertained; for the teaching of Jesus, important as it is, is *not* Christianity but the highest instance of Judaism. Jesus taught and thought as a Jew. He is for Christian faith something more than a distinguished exponent of the finest Jewish prophetic and ethical teaching. Any genuine acquaintance with the story of Christian thought will recognize that the message *about* Jesus—that in him, through him, and by him, the very activity of God is decisively at work in human experience—is different from the teaching *of* Jesus. If it were the latter alone, then the words of Samuel Taylor Coleridge would be to the point: 'If Christianity is ethics, then we should be followers of Socrates and not of Jesus Christ.'

I have dwelt on this matter, as on others in the preceding paragraphs, because I wish to urge upon any reader, whether an unordained person or one who has been given ordained ministerial function in the Church, precisely such a readiness for as much study as can be undertaken—and I urge this with a definitely pastoral interest, since surely we must all agree that authentic Christian faith is what we are supposed to communicate *and* that this communication can only be made when we are also aware of the ways of thinking which are present in our own day. Otherwise we shall either fail to speak christianly *or* we shall fail in 'getting across' the faith which is at the heart of the Church of Christ. The gospel does not exist in some airy region above the realm of human affairs. It has to do with down-to-earth realities; and in our day that includes the general knowledge, the science, and the problematic issues which we face and with which every human being must wrestle.

A person who keeps 'up-to-date' in this respect is not being disloyal to faithful Christian responsibility. On the contrary such a one is remembering the truth enunciated by St. Ambrose of Milan, centuries ago, who dared to say that 'every truth, wherever spoken, is spoken by the Holy Spirit.' This is why I venture to say that to a much larger degree than is commonly realized, the kind of Christian service, the quality of Christian witness, and the nature of Christian ministering, will be determined by the hard work which one is prepared to undertake, not only with the hands but with the head. Thoughtless and uninformed discipleship is unfaithful discipleship; it harms the person who indulges in it and it harms the people who might be won to Christian faith. The People of God deserve to have a membership, both ordained and unordained, which rejects shoddy thinking, negligence about facts, and hence meretriciousness in witness and teaching. The Good Shepherd cares for his sheep. Today, perhaps more than at any time in Christian history, that care demands of the undershepherds who are servants of God's servants the dedicated use of the human mind.

I wish to end this perhaps too extended discussion by observing that one of the purposes of what traditionally we call the Incarnation and the Atonement, was *not* to render unnecessary the use of our brains. We should use them to the best of our ability. God works in and through, if often in spite of, our limited mental capacity; we must be grateful that in his mercy he can and does do just this. But I can have no doubt that God also requires that his children, especially those who explicitly acknowledge him in Christian faith, shall fully use that mental capacity, however limited it may be, to his praise and glory—and for the good of all his children. Only when we have done as much as in us lies to obey that requirement can we honestly say that we have been dutiful in our discipleship. And only then have we the right to believe that God will be glad to make even that 'stupidity', which we acknowledge to be ours, to 'turn to his praise.'

When we come to understand this, we shall be prepared to give time to study, however simple this may be, knowing that to learn more of God's ways in the world, above all in the event of Jesus Christ and the response made to him in the community of faith, is an opportunity to be grasped with all our hearts. This is our obligation; it is also an occasion for joy.

Shepherding Christ's Flock

'To shepherd Christ's flock' is to be a pastor. And while that ministerial concern finds a special focus in the work of the ordained minister, the ordained priest of Christ, it is equally the task of each and every member of the Church as he or she fulfils the priesthood which is proper to a member of Christ's priestly Body.

As to the clergy, it is important that they take to heart the admonition of the great Puritan divine Richard Baxter, who wrote in *The Reformed Pastor*—one of the monuments of seventeenth century English literature—that their office is much more than 'those men have taken it to be, who think it consisteth in, preaching and administering the sacraments only.' Baxter was sure that the ordained minister was indeed to be a 'pastor' or shepherd on Christ's behalf; and this task included not only care for the people in his charge but also what in other traditions has been called 'the cure of souls' or, as nowadays we should very likely phrase it, the personal counseling of the people and the declaration to them of God's gracious forgiveness. Bishop Hensley Henson, the famous bishop of Durham in earlier years of this century, is said to have remarked that while an ordained minister would probably agree with you if you told him that he was not a brilliant preacher nor an able administrator, he would be deeply hurt if you told him that he was a bad pastor of his congregation.

The pastoral ministry is in a profound sense at the very heart of all ministry, whether this be the ministry of the parson, ordained to function for the Church in special ways, or the ministry of the Christian layperson who in his own style and manner should be committed to others in what today would be styled a 'caring' fashion. It is therefore important that we should consider what pastoral responsibility signifies and what are the wider functions which are included within that responsibility. And I can think of no better introduction to the subject than a longish quotation from a beautifully written book by Henry Scougal, a Scots divine of the eighteenth century. In this book, titled *The Importance and Difficulty of the Ministerial Function*, Scougal deals with just this subject. It is interesting that he speaks of 'ministerial function', thus anticipating the description of ministry which I have urged in this book.

Scougal addresses himself especially to what somebody has called 'the fledgling minister', the young ordained person; but what he says has its wider reference and is appropriately applied also to each Christian in his or her responsible concern for others, both within and without the bounds of the institutional Christian Church. Here is what he says:

'The great business of our calling is to advance the divine life in the world; to make religion sway and prevail; to frame and mould the souls of men into a conformity to God and superinduce the beautiful lineaments of his blessed image upon them; to enlighten their understanding and inform their judgements, rectify their wills and order their passions and sanctify all their affections.' He goes on to say, 'We are the instruments of God for effecting these great designs; and although we be not accountable for the success when we have done what lieth in our power, yet nothing below this should be our aim; and we should never cease our endeavours until that gracious change be wrought in every person committed to our charge' (*Works of Henry Scougal*, New York edition of 1846, pp. 206–7).

These words come from a generation long before our own and their language is not that which we should be likely to use; none the less, they set before us the great objectives of ordained pastoral work in the Christian Church and by extension are also applicable to the ministry of every Christian man or woman. I believe that we can profit greatly from giving them the most careful attention.

Scougal tells us that the 'great business' of ministering is 'to advance the divine life in the world.' We might rephrase this by saying that the purpose of the minister is to establish what the Ordinal (which I have already quoted) calls 'ripeness and perfectness of age in Christ.' The concern is to help towards the realization of 'life in Christ' which, as I have noted earlier in this book, is nothing other than 'life in love' because it is 'life in Love' (in God), as God has made himself known and available through Jesus Christ. When Scougal speaks of 'framing and moulding [our fellows] into a conformity to God' through 'superinducing the beautiful lineaments of [God's] blessed image' upon his human children, he is affirming that since Jesus Christ is the express Image of Deity, all humans who share in a common humanity are to be brought to 'conform' to that potentiality given them in their creation. This is the 'image' in which all are made, which by their sin and sloth they have damaged and marred, and which through Christ has once again been made possible for them, if only they will let him work his way in them.

A continual return in mind and will to this over-arching purpose—to the 'effecting of these great designs'—can do much to redeem the Christian vocation from its sometimes frustrating appearance of triviality and fussiness. We all know that we can do many tiresome things if we are sure that they are part of some great task. I recall a great Christian whom I once had the privilege of knowing well, who commented one day that 'a test of vocation to ministry is delight in doing humdrum things.' 'Delight' was a strong word in this connection, but it can become a true one when the right perspective is maintained.

Most ordained ministers can testify that a good deal of the work expected of them is indeed 'humdrum.' The sheep must be tended, so to say; and despite my comment on an earlier page, we must admit that often those sheep are 'silly', in the modern sense of that adjective; they do equally 'silly' things. The older meaning of 'silly' was 'innocent'; the contemporary meaning is foolish or ridiculous. Yet the sheep are not to be dismissed; they are to be loved and cared for. And when it comes to the caring shown by the non-ordained man or woman, to whom ministering is also a responsibility, the obligation to 'put up' with 'silliness' is equally great. Today we are aware of the truth of Bonhoeffer's statement that men and women have 'come of age'; they are no longer to be regarded as children but are to be treated as being at least relatively 'mature' in that they know their freedom, their responsibility, and their opportunity to become genuinely human. Yet at the same time, it is obvious that these moderns often value the wrong things and can be absurdly presumptuous in assuming human self-sufficiency for almost everything. And they are not without inanities and trivialities with which we must reckon. Yet they are people about whom the Christian must feel deep concern. 'Silly' things, as also triviality and inanities, may bring their problems. But they can also have their place, under God, in the 'affecting of the great designs' of the Good Shepherd whom we serve; and so they must be accepted without distress or irritation, perhaps even with a certain true joy.

My own experience as a teacher, who of choice as well as necessity must be in a pastoral relationship with my students, has led me to believe that once people are conscious that there is interest in them as persons, not as objects, they will often show a surprising (if sometimes exhausting) readiness to come for help. There is a long stream of them, of all shapes and sizes, so to say: men and women, girls and boys, with all sorts of problems and worries. If they know that somebody genuinely cares for them and is ready to be of assistance to them in their difficulties; if they feel that somebody loves them, in that she or he is ready to be at hand when their troubles are too heavy for them to bear; if they know that one is not quick to condemn their failures but eager to offer reassurance and do what is possible to assist them in their struggle to become more fully human; if they see that one is not 'judgmental' but redemptive in attitude—if they understand all this, they will come to one. I am sure that this particular personal aspect of ministry must be very dear to the heart of the Good Shepherd.

Nobody who understands the mission of the Church would deny that there are many wider issues to be faced. But I have come increasingly to think that this personal ministry is enormously important in our day. The more public and obvious concerns with good causes, civil agencies, social work, and the like are surely also the concern of the faithful Christian today. But what used to be called (as I have said) 'the cure of souls' is at the heart of ministering today, as it has always been in the history of the Christian Church. Very much to the point here is the parable of Jesus about the shepherd who goes out to seek and to find the one lost sheep. Unhappily, in our time it is not the one but the 'ninety and nine' who are lost. In an age when 'bigness' is so much emphasized, we may tend to think that the Christian minister, both ordained and unordained, should have a special call to the 'big' things; yet it was not so with our Master and our Pattern.

I must dwell on this theme. To know that somebody cares for *me:* that is what matters most to each one of us. If we talk and think a great deal about love, as a Christian must do, let us remember that love always *personalizes.* It does not deal with 'cases'; it deals with *people,* one by one. It does not think and talk about 'humanity at large'; it thinks and talks of this and that man or woman or child. G. K. Chesterton said that our Lord did not command us to love the human race but to love our fellow men and women. That means to care for each person as a person, not as one instance of a general class or category. Each is special; each is to be seen in her or his speciality. That requires us to single out, as it were, this or that particular one, that human being whom we meet as we go our way in the world. After all, we never meet 'humanity'; we meet this man, this woman, this child. Each of them has his or her own idiosyncracies, yet each also has a wonderful potentiality to become the child of God who can come to 'reflect the beautiful lineamants of [God's] blessed image.'

Once more I can be personal. One of the things which in recent years has been the special concern in my inadequate pastoral interest is perhaps unusual. I refer to the anxieties of the homosexual men and women in our society, persons who so often feel themselves rejected or condemned and frequently become bitter and hopeless. I have found that it is important to work for the general amelioration of the situation for homosexual persons in a broad sense; but I have also found that what is most needed, and when given most appreciated, is readiness to be accepting and caring for this or that human being who because of his or her particular sexual drive has great difficulty living in a society which is all too ready to reject, condemn, and even persecute. The 'big' cause should be furthered, to be sure; but the relation with this particular man or woman ought to make its claim upon us and it is with that single one that we can be most helpful.

Not only homosexual persons but many others today feel that they are 'lost in the crowd', as someone has phrased it. Who cares for each of them? Who will go to endless trouble for each of them? Surely the Christian, who has known something of the personalizing love of God, has a vocation to extend that love to the others whom he or she meets daily. Each is precious to God; and the only way in which this can be brought home is by letting each see that she or he is precious to Christian people. The ordained minister has a special obligation here; but so also the unordained Christian needs to recognize a similar obligation and to act upon it, to the fullest extent possible. If one genuinely believes, as a Christian must, that the universe pulses with love, then that love must be made visible and vital in the life of men and women. Thus to be the personalizing agent for the divine Charity is the highest vocation anybody could have. That vocation belongs to the Christian disciple; it cannot be avoided or neglected. And I need hardly add that if this is the general Christian vocation, it is in a way preeminently the vocation of the person who has been admitted to 'holy orders' as a functioning minister, in distinctive fashion, for the whole Body of Christ in its priestly nature.

In the seventeenth century in England, some Christian leaders showed a keen interest in the application of Christian moral principles and the 'spiritual' interpretation of life to the personal needs of individuals. Doubtless for that reason Richard Baxter, whom I have been quoting, devoted much time to what was in that period known as 'casuistical work.' This had obvious connections with the long Catholic tradition in which 'penitential theology' was an important aspect of the understanding of Christian ethics. It included, of course, the practice of private confession in the presence of a priest, with his declaration of 'pardon and absolution' for those who were truly penitent for their sins. But the English writers did not make the sharp distinction which in Roman Catholic circles tended to be made between 'moral theology' and the practice of confession, nor did they make what in those continental circles often seemed a too careful and neat apportioning of 'so much penance' for 'so much sin.' They did not see their task as the establishment of a precise balance between a person's moral responsibility and abstract moral standards. On the contrary, their major interest was in helping each person to grow 'in grace' as that person developed a fully-rounded life of faith, devotion, and conduct.

There has been a considerable revival of that sort of concern in most Christian denominations in recent years, including the regular use of 'the sacrament of absolution' (as it is often called today), with private confession and the declaration of divine pardon, or the Protestant use of what one American divine styled 'the minister's confessional.' Obviously interest in the availability for one or other of these is incumbent upon an ordained minister of the

Church; and many men and women have found that the use of this means of grace has been most helpful to them in their own Christian life. But there is also a genuine sense in which each Christian can serve in this sort of personal ministry, even if not with the 'authorization' of the Church such as appertains (at least in 'Catholic' communions) to the ordained person. Bonhoeffer used to insist, in the seminary which during Nazi days he directed in Germany, that those who were attending should 'confess to one another', thus further amplifying the conviction that every Christian is 'another Christ' (in St. Benedict's and Luther's language) to each fellow-Christian.

My concern here, however, is not with this practice so much as with the way in which we ought to help one another grow in our life of prayer or devotion. Not enough time has been spent, not enough effort has been made, to engage in a shared growth in praying, so that as 'they grow in age they may grow in grace and in the knowledge and love of our Saviour Jesus Christ.'

This responsibility creates a problem for many people today, since they are not at all sure what prayer really is. Some think that it hardly matters, anyway. And for a good number of Christian people, the understanding they have of prayer amounts to what Dean Inge once called 'pestering the deity with our petitions.' That biting description is not inaccurate if it is thought that prayer consists in nothing but requests made to God for what we happen to think we need or want. Indeed the whole business of prayer, both in theory and practice, needs serious rethinking today; and what is interesting, to some of us probably highly surprising, is that when such rethinking is undertaken, the result turns out to be very much what the old 'masters' of the devotional life have been saying for ages. What will emerge, I am sure, is the necessity for our making every effort to realize, in the sense of 'making real', the intentional relationship of each man and woman with God as the cosmic Lover. For prayer is essentially the willed identification of our own small desires for good with the great cosmic 'Desire-for-good' that is God. Along with this goes a growth in awareness of the reality of the divine Charity itself as pervasive throughout, yet unexhausted by, the created world of which we are a part. Thus a Christian is or ought to be one who is moving more and more toward 'life in Christ', so that (in Scougal's words) 'the divine life may have sway and prevail' in his or her human life.

Prayer is so important a part of the Christian discipline or pattern for living and is so much part of the ministerial vocation in its more pastoral aspect, that I now venture to speak about it at some length and shall return to it in the next chapter.

Very likely the current popularity of 'cults of reassurance', 'transcendental meditation', and oriental religious teaching is a consequence of a failure on the part of the Christian community of faith to offer the kind of assistance which men and women need if they are to deepen their awareness of God and find some enduring purpose in their lives. The response of responsible Christians ought not to be a cavalier rejection of such popularity but a recognition that it is incumbent upon members of Christ's Body to do much more to teach about and further the practice of prayer in the fullest Christian sense. These non-Christian movements quite plainly are meeting a need; but the need could be met much more satisfactorily by genuine Christian instruction in and exercise of the life of prayer. What is more, the difficulty with many of the cults is that they appear to be far too self-centered and in some instances are more likely to produce feelings of contentment and ease than genuinely Christian response in love and service toward others and in a deepening awareness of the reality of the God of suffering love. Or, more briefly, many of the cults fail to stress the Cross, objectively in history and subjectively in human experience. A devotion which is authentically Christian will focus on the revelation of God in the crucified (and of course the risen) Christ. Isaiah says, 'Thou shalt keep him in perfect peace whose mind is stayed on thee, because he trusteth in thee.' The practice of prayer, rightly understood and faithfully engaged in, can and does bring about a deep inner security which does not shirk the harsh facts of human existence nor the passion of God in Christ. But to know God's gracious action for us requires that the mind *is* 'stayed' on God; and that cannot happen simply by talking about it or wishing that it might be so. There is hard work—a sharing in God's passion—involved in genuine Christian prayer.

Of course much conventional talk about prayer and praying will not be useful for us today. By this I mean much the same as did Bishop John Robinson when in one of his books he protested against the almost mechanical instruction about it which he received in his theological college as a young man. What was wrong about it, he said, was that it seemed altogether too much a matter of escaping from the world into some heavenly region where he could be 'alone with God.' But as Teilhard de Chardin, not to mention many others like Michael Quoist, has taught us, 'escapist prayer'$ is not genuinely Christian. When we attend to God—the God who is always with us but to whom, because we have so much to do each day, we do not always give our attention—we are not running away from the world which he is creating, which he dearly loves, and in which he is unceasingly active and at work. Rather, we are seeking to raise that world, as we 'lift up our hearts', so that everything in it may be suffused with his consciously known and consciously felt reality. And as we have opportunity, we ought to help other people to grasp this fact, so that their praying may be realistic and penetrating in its interest in the created order, in their fellow humans who live here, and in dedication to the continuing service we all should give to God as he works in his children.

I remember a student who found that prayer was becoming burdensome and meaningless. He consulted me about this problem. After much thought and discussion, we concluded that the difficulty was that the sort of praying he had been led to use was so remote from his daily concerns that it appeared irrelevant. I was bold enough to suggest that for a short time, until things got better for him, he should give up 'formal' prayer and simply trust to God as he said little 'arrow prayers'—about which I shall speak in the sequel. What I recommended was for *him,* not for everybody. Some people need desperately a more formal pattern of prayer; they need a 'scheme' which will give their praying an orderly quality. Others will be helped by using books like John Baillie's splendid *Diary of Prayer,* published many years ago and recently re-issued in a cheap edition which is readily available. But whatever experience and experiment may show to be best for any one of us, no Christian can fail to 'attend to God', as the old writers used to say, and to do this at a time when and a place where he or she can be quiet and able to 'recollect God' without fuss or worry.

I conclude this discussion of prayer by repeating what was said at an earlier stage—namely, that we shall find that much which modern experience can provide by way of an understanding of prayer is very similar to the way in which the old masters and teachers of Christian devotion understood it. Stress will be on 'attention' to God as actively present with his children; on 'the elevation of the spirit to God' (with St. John Damascene and St. Thomas Aquinas); on the 'sacrament of the present moment' and 'surrender to divine providence' (with Père Jean de Caussade, lately translated into English by Kitty Muggeridge); and on the use both of the 'Jesus prayer' of the Eastern Church (a simple regular repetition of the words, 'Jesus, Son of God, have mercy upon me, a sinner') or of so-called 'arrow prayers' (in which from time to time the address to God of brief 'ejaculations' occurs, such as 'My God, I love thee', or 'Lord, I give myself to thee', or 'Help me, O Lord in [this or that situation])'. In the next chapter I shall say more about this whole subject, one that to my mind is most frequently neglected yet most plainly needed: how, when, for what, and why we should engage in prayer, so that we may become men and women who truly live 'in Love' and are deeply concerned for our human comrades.

It will be remembered that Scougal spoke in these words: 'Though we be not accountable for the success . . . yet nothing below this should be our aim; and we should never cease our endeavours until that gracious change is wrought. . . .' What 'change'? The answer is given by Scougal himself in our quotation from him: that each of us shall come to know 'the superinducement upon them of the beautiful lineaments of [God's] blessed image.' Surely, then, our first interest must always be our increasing conformation of ourselves and others to God as known in Christ. *That* is the end or purpose of praying.

There is much else which should have attention in a chapter devoted to pastoral ministering with and for and by the People of God. I shall speak of only one or two matters which seem to deserve particular consideration.

One has to do with 'vocation.' Thanks to the use of that word in secular circles where it is taken to mean choice of some 'career' which may provide a livelihood for a man or woman, a misunderstanding has arisen in religious discussion. In main-line Christianity there is but *one* Christian vocation. That is not the ordained ministry, as 'career counselors' have often assumed. The one and only *Christian* vocation is the call to be a human being, coming to full human existence as response is made to the 'call' of God in Christ. Put briefly, it is the call to holiness—not to a 'better than thou' sort of character, but to a relationship with God, known in Christ, in which 'the process of Christ' (as we saw that William Law phrased it) is accomplished in everyone who dares to 'profess and call himself [or herself] Christian', to use the language of *The Book of Common Prayer.*

One implication of this central and single vocation is that it may express itself in a great variety of ways. Hence there are 'specialized ministries', not only for those who are ordained but for every servant of Christ. Each one of us must ask and answer the question: 'How can I exercise my "vocation and ministry"; in what particular field and in what particular way can I best do this?' Sometimes the area of action will be in what is known as 'the secular world'; sometimes it will be in those kinds of effort which are commonly denominated 'religious'; sometimes it will be in a mixture of the two, like teaching in a Christian school or some similar work.

Whatever may be the choice prayerfully and thoughtfully made, such fields should be ones that provide the opportunity for real Christian witness. My own work has been in teaching; I know that what Scougal said can become a major concern for a teacher who is prepared not only to do his best in his given task as this is set before him but also in helping students to understand the meaning of faith and to become, so far as lies in them, true men and women 'in Christ.' It is likely that in the future there will be much more 'secular ministering' by Christian people. Nor is this to be regretted as somehow unfaithful. On the contrary, it is a way of claiming, for the Lover who is God, more and more of human life in more and more places and ways.

For this reason it is all the more necessary that we let our minds dwell upon the call to serve God in whatever work is ours. The ordained person knows this, if that person has responded with genuine dedication to his particular function in the life of the Body of Christ. The unordained man or woman must equally respond, in his or her own way, to the same responsibility; he or she must also let the mind dwell on this vocation. Yet in doing so they ought first of all turn their minds to the Good Shepherd who looked out for and sought to bring those who were 'lost' to the love which is their possibility. Not success, but faithfulness, is what counts. The old language about 'shepherding the Lord's flock' may seem quaint today, yet the truth it states can never grow stale. To be our Lord's agent in the doing of his salvific work is our privilege, whether we happen to have had 'hands laid upon us' in ordination or whether we happen to be ordinary baptized members of Christ who have promised to be his 'soldiers and servants unto [our] life's end.'

We should be the more ready to dwell on those scenes in the gospel where Jesus is portrayed as the Shepherd, with his loving care for each who came to him with some need or whom he found in such need long before they thought of what he might mean to (and do for) them. In his acts as in his words Jesus was the expression of a Love which will not let go of anybody. The under-shepherd is to reflect something of that divine Love.

Finally, each of us knows the need for the grace of God—the divine Love in act towards and with us—so that he or she may thus reflect that image which in Christ is expressly visible among us. This is why we pray that 'Christ may dwell in us and we in Christ'; this is why we yearn to follow the pattern of his shepherding care for others, not so much for our own sakes as for the sake of the men and women whom God in Christ so deeply and dearly loves.

God's Servants for God's People:
'Men and Women of God'

I do not much like the conventional phrase, often applied solely to the ordained clergy, that they are to be 'men of God.' Surely, if the argument of this book has any validity, *every* one of us is intended to be a man or woman 'of God.' Certainly everybody who dares to think of himself or herself as a Christian has that calling. Alas, the term sometimes also carries with it a lugubrious association, as in cartoons in which the artist may portray an ordained minister in absurd situations or looking like an undertaker of the gloomier sort who dispenses spurious good cheer to the bereaved or troubled. None the less, I have decided to use the phrase in this chapter, because it does in fact point to the requirement that a Christian, whatever his or her role in the Church's life, should be so much 'in God' and 'of God' that others may be drawn in that same direction.

Obviously the representative and functional ordained minister of the Christian Church is not the only one to whom the term should be applied, however popular may be that usage. All God's children, whether within or without the Christian fellowship, are meant to belong to God and hence to become men and women *for* God, with those 'blessed lineaments', of which Scougal wrote, plainly marked upon them. All Christian people, morever, are to be for God and of God *in Christ;* they should be moving towards making actual their humanity in a love which reflects and acts for the divine Love which in Jesus Christ is enacted in human history. The job of the ordained pastor or priest is precisely to work towards that end for the persons committed to his care and as himself functioning in a particular way as an undershepherd of the Good Shepherd whom he, like all Christ's people, represents.

Perhaps there *is* a special propriety in describing the ordained person in this way, as 'man of God.' Such a person, by the fact of ordination, stands for, and by the grace of God is permitted to make real for others, the truth that they are all of them God's children, God's men and women, God's beloved, Christ's flock, Christ's sheep. Thus, within the Christian Church the ordained person must ever be a visible sign of what ought to be the case with every one of that Church's members. He placards before the world the possibility, available for all, of a life in and with God which is to be shared as widely as it can be shared.

In this chapter I wish first to consider what in the preceding chapter I spoke of as 'the call to holiness.' Now that kind of call, that vocation to the reality of 'holiness', is the call to an intimate relationship with God. I do not apologize for using the old word 'holiness' and its synonym 'sanctity.' I am not talking about sanctimoniousness or about a negative variety of holiness, which are both of them horrible things and which should have no place in Christian life. They put people off, and rightly so; and if I may presume to speak for God, they must put God off too! They are the expression of an attitude to existence in which the whole of life is centered in oneself and in one's presumed superiority over others. We should avoid them as the poisonous things they are. Genuine holiness and real sanctity are quite different.

I think that here, as in earlier instances, we can find a helpful and sound approach through a book written a long time ago. Thomas Wilson was the Bishop of Sodor and Man during the eighteenth century. The great schoolmaster Thomas Arnold thought that Wilson was one of the most important of English divines; his son, the poet and essayist, Matthew Arnold, came to share his father's high estimation of the bishop. The best-known of Thomas Wilson's writing is called *Meditations on his Sacred office,* intended originally for newly-ordained clergymen. As we shall see, much that Wilson says in that book is equally applicable to the unordained man or woman who is a member of the Christian Church.

In one of his discussions, Bishop Wilson considers what he thinks to be the 'ideal' which should be held before every minister of Christ. He writes in these words: 'Fervency in devotion; frequency in prayer; aspiring after the love of God continually, striving to get above the world and the body; loving silence and solitude, as far as one's condition will permit; humble and affable to all; patient in suffering affronts and contradictions; glad of occasions of doing good even to enemies; doing the will of God and promoting his honour to the utmost of one's power; resolving never to offend him willingly, for any temporal pleasures, profit, or loss.'

With some of these phrases we today cannot be too happy; many of his words are hardly applicable or helpful to us. The sharp distinction which the bishop draws between the laity and the ordained ministry, about which I have given no quotations, and the somewhat negative attitude toward 'the world and the body', as if these were not part of God's creation and intended to be enjoyed as a means for God's service yet without misuse for personal profit or gain: here are some of the things which we should wish to reject. Yet to my mind the first three clauses in the quotation are deserving of our close attention: 'fervency in devotion; frequency in prayer; striving after the love of God continually.' Surely these words tell us that as dedicated Christians we must be those whose devotion is eager or 'fervent', whose praying is a frequent and not a merely occasional exercise, and who ceaselessly aspire to realize in our lives the reality of the love of God towards us and our responsive love to him. At least in intention, we may say, these are what should mark the life of everyone who ventures to 'profess and call himself [or herself] Christian'. To labour for such a quality of life is to be the mark which characterizes each of us. This is our Christian vocation and we cannot and should not seek to evade it.

In our seeking to become a man or woman 'of God', we can find assistance in some of the ancient customs of the Christian Church as these have been developed down the centuries. For example, in the matter of our daily praying, we can learn to use and appreciate the formal 'daily offices' of the Christian Church. In an older time, and still today in Roman Catholic, Eastern Orthodox, Lutheran and Anglican books of common prayer, there is such a 'daily office', traditionally known as the *Opus Dei* or 'Work of

God'. Here there are readings, prayers, canticles, psalms, and other material which during the course of the year cover pretty well the whole round of Christian faith and devotion. To use those 'offices' will benefit any Christian, whether ordained or unordained. Every ordained priest of the Church of England is directed, in the rules which indicate his duty (found in the Prayer Book), to 'say' Mattins and Evensong daily; a similar direction is found in the Roman and Eastern Orthodox communions. Lutherans are increasingly doing exactly the same thing. But in any Christian denomination there are collections of ancient and hallowed prayers which provide guidance and assistance for the Christian believer. The Presbyterian Book of Common Order is an instance, from among those who follow a less liturgical routine of worship. The value of such material is that it promotes a balanced approach to the life of prayer, with due regard for the great festivals, the important moments of recollection, and the acts of celebration which are to mark the life in grace. They will help to 'order' or pattern our praying.

Some time for praying is available every day. How that praying is done is a matter of personal need and requirement. Some will do this in one way, others in a different way. *How* does not matter so much as that praying is genuinely a part of the life of the faithful Christian. Something must be said, later in this chapter, about such praying, especially in what is called 'personal' prayer. For the moment, I wish only to stress that prayer, defined by a friend of mine as essentially 'thinking devoutly', is not an incidental but an essential aspect of Christian existence.

In the Holy Communion we have of course the chief act of Christian worship. Attendance at this sacrament is not only a requirement of all Christian groups in the 'Catholic' tradition; more and more it is recognized as equally a requirement for those in the Reformed churches. In the agelong tradition of the Christian Church, the Eucharist has more and more become the focal point of worship; hence it has also become a clue to the entire life of prayer. It complements and fulfils personal praying; personal praying flows naturally from eucharistic celebration. Surely an ordained minister will wish to lead others to share in the sacrament with great frequency; surely every Christian, ordained or unordained, will wish to be present at—'to assist at', as the old phrase has it—the sacramental celebration as often as possible.

We have mentioned prayer and sacrament. There is also the examination of conscience, with the confession to God of what is wrong with us. This too is part of the agelong tradition of the Church. In such examination of self, it is important to avoid what Baron von Hügel once called 'a spiritual flea-hunt', with concentration on minutiae and with an overly-scrupulous attitude—these certainly are unhealthy and can readily produce an unpleasant sort of hyper-critical mentality that is dangerous to growth in genuine loving of God and our fellow-humans. But facing up to oneself, in the light of God's self-sacrificing love displayed on Calvary, is both a desirable and shaming exercise. If one looks at the Cross and then looks at one's own life, there will be an inevitable awareness of inadequacy and defection, much more real and shaming than any amount of spiritual 'bookkeeping.' For sin is not the violation of a set of rules laid down to be obeyed; it is the violation of a relationship between God and humankind, and between humans, which damages seriously the openness of love and the obedient surrender which is our 'reasonable service.'

In some Christian circles—those which also have the 'daily office'—there is provision for such examination to be followed by confession in the presence of an ordained priest of the Church. That minister is then to declare God's forgiveness to the person who is duly penitent for wrong doings. Today it is recognized that on some occasions, if not always, the same sort of confession may be made to a fellow Christian, whether ordained or not. I have mentioned how Dietrich Bonhoeffer wrote about this when he told how in the seminary which he directed during the Nazi regime in Germany, the young people who were in his charge were encouraged to engage in just this kind of confession; they could then receive, from their brother or sister in Christ, the assurance of divine acceptance and forgiveness. It is worth noting again that the famous American Protestant preacher Harry Emerson Fosdick did some of his most effective pastoral work in what he styled 'the minister's confessional.' It is good for all of us, now and again, to speak to such an ordained minister or to a fellow-Christian, about our Christian life. The Wesleys originated the old Methodist 'class-meeting', where small groups of believers met regularly to help each other through mutual confession as well as through reporting on their sense of growth towards 'the perfection' that is in Christ Jesus. They were wise in establishing such opportunities.

We may now turn to the more directly personal life of devotion. Bishop Wilson urged that we are to aspire 'after the love of God continually.' Here is our deepest vocation; and here too is the aim which should be ours as we seek to become faithful ministering agents, whether ordained or unordained, of the divine activity ceaselessly at work toward human wholeness. Participation in the regular round of worship, including the Holy Communion; use of some pattern or order for praying; readiness to examine oneself and confess what has been wrong about our lives . . . all this; and also prayer when one is by oneself, in one's own place, and at one's own selected time. Without some such personal devotion, the more public expression of devotion may become routine, a 'matter of habit.' Of course there is nothing wrong with habits, if they are *good* habits; but we need to dig down deeper into our own existence for the establishment of a more direct relationship with God as Love. I wish to make six suggestions which may be of assistance in this matter.

First, such praying should be *one's own*. That is, it must be an honest personal effort, in which each of us seeks after God and responds to the One who is always seeking us. Reliance on other people's prayers will be of great assistance here; it can also be somewhat dangerous if it becomes a substitute for the honest expression of one's own strong desires and the willed identification of one's own life with the Love that is God, and doing this in a fashion which is appropriate to each person in his or her particular situation.

In such personal praying, the whole range of prayer may have its place. In another book, *Praying Today* (Eerdmans, 1974), I have tried to present this wide range and to indicate something of 'the theology of prayer' and the methods which may be followed. Here I shall not pursue this topic, but shall proceed at once to my second point, which is that our praying should always be genuinely *Christian* praying.

We need to get out of our minds, and therefore get out of our praying, the many sub-christian concepts of God that are often found even among devout Christian people. To conceive of God as sheer power, or as moral despot, or as ruthless in his demands, or as remote ruler, or as basically unaffected by what happens in the creation, is to conceive of God in a fashion which denies or minimizes the Christian understanding that God's 'nature and his name is Love', as Charles Wesley's great hymn puts it. There is all the difference in the world between prayer as cringing submission to power, servile anxiety in the divine presence, anxious observance of rules, and the like, and prayer with the awe and reverence which are appropriate to our being in the presence of One whose love 'will not let me go.' If prayer is what John Damascene in the early Church called it, 'the elevation of the mind to God', then it will not resemble behaviour in an oriental sultan's court; it will be more familial and more intimate. It will be prayer marked by adoration and thanksgiving, to be sure; it will be prayer of confession for one's sin; it will be expression of desire and aspiration. But above all it will be the bringing of ourselves and those whom we remember into the 'attentive presence of God', as one old devotional writer (Challoner) put it. It will be the opening of self so that we may be purified and used by God to effect his purpose of love and his will for justice in the concrete realities of this world. In other words, it will not be an 'escape-mechanism.'

Christian praying, for ordained minister and for lay person, is primarily to be understood as the urgent desire for 'the increase of faith, hope, and charity', as the old collect for 14 Trinity puts it. The way to this increase, as the same collect indicates, is through our learning to 'love that which [God] commands.' That word 'commands' means, in this context, the situation or place in which each of us has his or her human existence. Hence praying consists in *the active acceptance* of God's will; and this is my third point.

In the Garden of Gethsemane, we are told in the gospels, Jesus prayed 'Not my will but thine be done.' The stress in that saying comes on the words 'be done.' Jesus was not gloomily submitting himself to an inexorable fate. Rather, he was opening himself, fully and completely, in order to become the effectual instrument for God to use, thus playing his essential part in the divine activity in the world. This was active acceptance, not passive acquiescence. A clue to that kind of acceptance is to be found in a book by a French Jesuit, Jean de Caussade, who lived in the seventeenth and early eighteenth centuries. This writer (to whom I referred in the last chapter) had much to say about what he styled 'the sacrament of the present moment', where God is recognized as actively present in any given moment of our lives. To that present-ness of God, he urged, the faithful person will surrender himself or herself. Hence his book is given the title *Abandonment to Divine Providence*. This title does not sound very attractive in the English language; but the French meaning is that one surrenders or commits oneself totally to God seen here and now and where one is in time and place.

Consider what that implies. We have but one 'time' in which we can know and love God and thus receive the 'increase' for which we hope. That time is *now*, in the 'present moment.' Here we can respond to God's loving movement towards us. Here we can let ourselves be opened to the divine action for us, with us, in us, and upon us. Here we can learn to be obedient to God's loving will. Thus genuinely Christian praying is not the attempt to twist God's purposes to suit our wishes but the strong desire to let our purposes be conformed to *his*. If we bear this in mind and approach our times of personal prayer with this in view, we shall have the right perspective. We shall not spend so much of our time telling God what we think we want nor shall we exhaust ourselves by an overly-scrupulous fussing about our sins. That we *are* sinners is indeed the case; but we should not focus our attention on it. Our focus is always to be on *God,* in his beauty and goodness and care. In so doing we seek to make it our constant endeavor to allow the life of Christ to become our own life.

A good deal of unnecessary difficulty has been caused by popular talk about prayer as 'speaking to God' and then expecting God to 'speak to us.' But this is far too *verbal* a view of the matter. Prayer, on the contrary, is not a matter of talking so much as it is a waiting upon God, an openness to God, and a surrender to God. It is not a continual chattering but an enjoyment of God and a uniting of our tiny desire for good with his enormously strong desire for good. This is somewhat like the best moments of our human relationships. Talking, in all awe and reverence for the other, is certainly part of this relationship; but it is not the heart of the thing. The 'being in the presence' is what is central to human caring. In any event, God's way of speaking to his children is not by verbal communication but by activity and present-ness. The Bible makes this clear in its continual stress on divine action in history and experience. A story told about a French peasant illustrates the point. He was seen sitting in Church, simply looking at the crucifix above the altar. When asked what he was doing he replied, 'I look at him and he looks at me.' By such self-exposure to God in his loving and demanding activity we do not 'become' God; but we are conformed to him, so that the divine love (supremely enacted in the event of Jesus Christ) is reflected in us and at work within us and through us. This is the Christian's aim; this is the Christian's deep intention.

The fourth point that I make here has to do with *our making time to pray.* The old gospel-hymn says, 'Take time to be holy'; and it is correct in what it tells us. Obviously we should not be like a man whom I once knew, who kept me and two companions waiting for nearly an hour while he finished his daily meditation before telephoning to a repairman to release us from a damaged lift in the block of flats. This was silly. In an odd way, it also was lacking in charity. None the less, a Christian must find the time—make the time, if necessary—for prayer, for the reading of books of devotion or 'spiritual reading', for the study of the Bible, and for meditation on God's revealing action for his children. It requires effort for any of us to learn to 'think prayerfully about God', as an old friend of mine once defined his own practice of prayer and devotion.

Simplicity, straightforwardness, and honesty in prayer, with the right Christian perspective, and the sincere attempt to find time for our praying: these are all necessary for the Christian man or woman who hopes to become 'a man or a woman of God.' I may note here that I myself found, over a long period, that a book already mentioned, John Baillie's little book *Diary of Prayer,* published many years ago by Oxford University Press and in print continuously since that time, was a great help to me, even though it was compiled, not by a fellow-Anglican, but by a distinguished Scots Presbyterian divine! There is nothing in that book which I have had to *unpray,* so to speak; and that was a tremendous boon.

Each of us can also find helpful the compilation of our own forms and sequences of prayer, in addition to any outside help we use. This compilation will enable us to have our own special prayers which may come from many different sources; and thus our daily exercise will indeed become our very own. And naturally we shall try to read the works of some of the great masters of prayer; to find these it may be helpful to consult a pastor or friend whose familiarity with them is greater than our own.

How *long* should one pray? *When* during the day should one pray? These are questions which do not permit of a general answer, since all will depend on our particular possibilities and even more on what von Hügel called our own *attrait*—the way in which each of us personally is drawn to the practice of prayer and the amount of time for it that we find helpful. But time must be found, as must a place where we can pray undisturbed. Some will be most benefited by short periods at different times of the day; others will prefer longer consecutive periods. Nobody can prescribe for others on matters such as this.

My fifth point is that while personal prayer must always be one's own, there is also a sense in which *Christian* prayer can never be that. For no Christian can consider himself or herself as being unrelated to the people around them and to the needs of the world. These people and those needs must be borne in mind; they must be brought by us to the heart of God as that heart has been disclosed in Christ. In a way, we are always praying for others and for the world's needs, since as a Christian each of us represents God's love for his creation and this means that we are (what an ancient writer styled) 'creation's priests to God.' Even when others are not specifically in mind, this remains true. Tennyson's well-known lines apply to our Christian praying: 'And so the whole round world is every way/ Bound by gold chains about the feet of God.'

As a sixth and last point, we should recognize that the continuing practice of prayer will help us when we must go through deep waters. No human being, certainly no Christian, can escape the occasional sense of dereliction; nor should such an one wish to do so, since the Lord we adore himself had his time of despair as he hanged on the Cross. How are we to meet such times?

A little remembered novel by a writer of an earlier generation, Mrs. Humphrey Ward, has in it a paragraph which I greatly like. In this book, called *The Case of Richard Meynell*, Mrs. Ward tells the story of a clergyman who is beset by personal tragedy and by the opposition of his superiors in the Church. He is almost ready to give up his ministry, perhaps even to deny his Christian faith. 'Now,' writes Mrs. Ward, 'there descended upon him the darkest hour of his history. It was simply a struggle for existence on the part of all those powers of the soul that make for action, against the forces that make for death and inertia. It lasted long; and it ended in the slow and difficult triumph, the final ascendancy of the "Yeas" of life over the "Nays." . . . He won the difficult fight, not as a philosopher, but as a Christian impelled, chastened, brought into line again, by purely Christian memories and Christian ideas. The thought of Christ healed him, gradually gave him courage to bear the agony of self-criticism, self-reproach, that was none the less overwhelming because his calmer mind, looking on, knew it to be irrational . . . There was a solemn kneeling by the Cross; a solemn opening of the mind to the cleansing and strengthening forces that flow from that life and death which are Christianity's central possession: the symbol through which, now understood in this way, now in that, the Eternal speaks to the Christian soul.'

Probably most of us are not likely to face the sort of struggle which Mrs. Ward represents her hero as undergoing. But the *point* is there; it is there for every Christian, ordained or unordained. Precisely when we are attacked by 'the forces that make for death and inertia'; when in consequence we suffer from 'the self-criticism and self-reproach' which 'the calmer mind, looking on', knows to be irrational; when we are in the depths which our Lord himself knew when he cried, 'My God, my God, why hast thou forsaken me?'—precisely then the whole of our life of prayer, with all of our 'purely Christian memories and ideas', will come to our aid. Then we too will be able to know 'the solemn kneeling by the Cross', with the 'solemn opening of the mind to the cleansing and strengthening forces' which are to be found in him who is 'the symbol through which the Eternal speaks to the Christian soul.'

Hence we do well to meditate much on that Cross where incarnate Love gave himself for the life of the world. We do well to keep ourselves turned, as George Tyrrell once said, 'to that strange Man on his Cross', remembering, as Tyrrell also said, that his arms are 'spread wide, not for some select few, but for the whole of the *orbis terrarum.*' We do well to center our thoughts and wills and affections there, where the Good Shepherd gave his life for the sheep. In him, who is the express Image of God in man, who is true God enacted for us in a true Man, we have our pattern and are given the power we need, as well as the right perspective on human existence. Unless we have come to know him well, through our 'fervency in devotion, frequency in prayer'; and '[our] aspiring after' the God of love made visible in him, we shall hardly be able to meet such situations as Mrs. Ward portrayed or the less tragic ones which we ourselves must encounter. We may even make shipwreck of our basic Christian vocation and our call to minister in his name, whether we be ordained or unordained Christian men and women.

But this failure need not be. Nor will it be, if we have constantly sought, again in Bishop Wilson's words, to 'do the will of God and promote his honour to the utmost of our power,' if we have indeed been constant in prayer so that Christ is formed in us and we live in him and he in us. Then, although it is likely that *we* shall never know it, others will take notice of us, that we 'have been with Jesus.' We shall be like the Good Shepherd and shall reflect his character and his concerns. Surely we could want no other reward than to be 'like him, as he is.'

Afterword

In this book I have discussed a variety of Christian concerns, with the focus on the way in which each member of the Church, ordained or unordained, has been called to serve in Christ's ministry. My purpose has been to indicate that we are all of us ministering servants of God in Christ and of God's people for Christ. I have urged that there is no impassable gulf between the ordinary member of the Church and the person who has been ordained for a specific function within the broader ministerial functioning proper to the Body of Christ. And I have sought to show that in that broader functioning each of us who 'professes and calls himself' or herself Christian has a part and place.

I realize that there are some areas of Christian concern which have not been given the attention they deserve. The responsibility for 'liberation', for example, has been barely touched upon. Nobody who is aware of the Christian imperative can forget that millions of God's children are oppressed, rejected, impoverished and neglected by 'the powers that be.' Not only in Latin America and the 'Third World' is this the case; in parts of the world which have been highly privileged there are many men and women who cry out for liberation, even if for historical reasons they believe that the Christian Church is unlikely to be of much assistance to them in their need. I have not discussed this pressing concern, however, largely because my own contacts and experience have not been such as to provide me with the necessary information. Yet like many others I am keenly conscious of the problem and anxious to do all that I can, in my own situation, to help in this task. And there are other areas, too, which have not received the attention which a full and adequate discussion of ministering by the Christian Church would require.

But I am convinced that the approach which I have taken, with its continual insistence on the mission of the Church to bring God's love in Christ to all men and women, points the way to a proper understanding of Christian concern in every area and aspect of human experience. Another instance, of course, would be the growing awareness of what is called 'the ecological crisis'; so would be the need for striving after disarmament among the nations, the rejection of nuclear warfare, and much else in a world that is desperately in need of a vision of peace with justice, informed by the spirit of loving care and open to new ways in which that peace with justice may be established among us.

My own distinctive work within the Christian community has been in the field of theological statement. In the second chapter I asserted the importance, indeed the necessity, of such work today, as in every age of Christian history. One thing seems clear, to me at any rate. This is the need for the re-conception of the theological implications of our common faith in God actively at work in the world and supremely self-expressed, so far as we Christians are concerned, in the historical reality to which we point when we say 'Jesus Christ.' I believe that for far too long Christian thinkers have been content to work with what I style other 'models' for God, and hence with patterns of Christian thought, which are less than adequately Christian. They have not seen that within the community of faith we have been too acquiescent in portrayals of God which have no claim to Christian acceptance. They have failed to recognize that what has been given us in what Whitehead called 'the brief Galilean vision', the event of Jesus Christ, must provide the one inescapable criterion for Christian thought, Christian worship, Christian life, and the way in which the Christian fellowship (whose origin is in that decisive event) should understand itself and its mission in the world.

Only when we have the right ordering of our thinking on such matters can we expect to have the right understanding of what our ministering is to be like. If we have pictured God as an arbitrary dictator, it is inevitable that we shall look at the Church as speaking and working with condescension; in the French phrase, *de haut en bas,* looking down upon and deigning to interest itself in the world's affairs. If we think of God as like some oriental ruler whose subjects cringe before him in servile submission, we shall engage in worship and service in a fashion appropriate to such a picture. If our picture of God is of the kind of moral ruler who has established laws that bear little if any resemblance to the concrete realities of human experience, we are likely to teach and live a Christianity which is rigid, unsympathetic, lacking in compassion, and demanding unquestioning obedience to supposedly divine demands that are often more than humankind can obey. On the other hand, a portrayal of God which represents him as sentimental, so benign that he has no unswerving purpose and no faithfulness to divine demands for the best that men and women can offer, is likely to turn the Church into an irrelevant community in a world which needs people with conviction and who are ready to give their entire allegiance to God as the 'rightness' which constitutes 'the grain of the universe.' But contrariwise, a picture of God which sees deity as utterly masculine in the pejorative sense of aggressive and with none of the tenderness which we associate with the feminine in our experience, will lead us to assume that the Christian fellowship is to be characterized by what nowadays is styled *machismo*—it will be the unsympathetic, rigorous, self-reliant, unyielding sort of society which self-righteously spends its time in telling men and women what is wrong with them, apparently delighting in condemnation and rejection.

To grasp the truth disclosed in the 'Galilean vision' is to be aware of a quite different divine reality. God is then known to be the 'cosmic Lover', as I delight in phrasing it. In that phrase, the word 'cosmic' indicates that God's concern is universal, related to everything and caring for everyone; and the word 'lover' indicates that the application of this divine concern is particular, directed toward each and every part of the world in its own specific character, with its own specific potentiality, and in its own specific time and place. Furthermore, cosmic Love is no sentimental, easy going, undemanding activity; on the contrary it shows what C. S. Lewis once called 'a severe mercy', with both generosity of spirit and insistence on the best that can be done in every instance of created existence.

This is not the place to present a full-orbed theological interpretation of what has just been said. In other books I have written about such matters; and I venture, with what I hope is a becoming modesty, to refer readers to some of these books—including especially a treatment of God's grace (*Abounding Grace*, Mowbrays 1981) and *Picturing God* (SCM Press, 1982). But I believe that a consequence of our taking with utmost seriousness the vision of God as 'pure unbounded Love', known as exactly that through the decisive divine action in human existence in the Man Jesus, will mean that our theology will have to undergo a radical revision; that our worship will have to be re-ordered (here the recently revised Book is of great importance as a step in that direction); and that our moral teaching will have to be both more insistent on love-in-act, on justice among nations and among persons, and on the necessity for self-giving as the key-motif in human existence—and also more ready to recognize that contemporary life cannot be governed by a pattern that may have been appropriate in other ages but in our time is seen as repressive and unworkable.

None the less, the abiding truth is still found in the Christian 'thing', as G. K. Chesterton called it. The task of ministering remains constant, the widest sharing in that ministry is still to be stressed, and the ordained minister still has a specific function to perform on behalf of the priesthood of the Body of Christ which he represents and for which he acts. In each new age Christian identity stands firm, although often the ways in which it manifests itself may be different. God is the one faithful reality, although precisely in God's being faithful we shall see that Isaiah was correct in saying that God 'does new things.' God calls his servants, those who are under-shepherds of the Good Shepherd, who are workers with him towards reconciliation and abundant life (or *shalom* which is harmonious and rightly patterned existence), to realize their true vocation—and having realized what that vocation requires, to act upon it loyally, faithfully, humbly and courageously.